Jerry on Jerry

The Unpublished Jerry Garcia Interviews

Jerry Garcia, 1987.

Jerry on Jerry

The Unpublished Jerry Garcia Interviews

Edited by Dennis McNally

Foreword by Trixie Garcia

BLACK DOG
& LEVENTHAL
PUBLISHERS
NEW YORK

Black Dog & Leventhal Publishers
Hachette Book Group
1290 Avenue of the Americas
New York, NY 10104

www.blackdogandleventhal.com
Printed in the United States of America
Cover and interior design by OhioBoy Art & Design

WOR

First Edition: November 2015
10 9 8 7 6 5 4 3 2 1

Black Dog & Leventhal Publishers is an imprint of Hachette Books, a division of Hachette Book Group. The Black Dog & Leventhal Publishers name and logo are trademarks of Hachette Book Group, Inc.

The Hachette Speakers Bureau provides a wide range of authors for speaking events. To find out more, go to www.HachetteSpeakersBureau.com or call (866) 376-6591.

The publisher is not responsible for websites (or their content) that are not owned by the publisher.

Library of Congress Cataloging-in-Publication Data

Garcia, Jerry, 1942-1995.

Jerry on Jerry : the unpublished Jerry Garcia interviews / edited by Dennis McNally ; foreword by Trixie Garcia. -- First edition.

pages cm

Includes index.

ISBN 978-0-316-38959-4 (hardcover) -- ISBN 978-1-4789-3167-6 (audio download) -- ISBN 978-1-4789-3166-9 (audio cd) 1. Garcia, Jerry, 1942-1995--Interviews. 2. Rock musicians--United States--Interviews. 3. Grateful Dead (Musical group) I. McNally, Dennis, editor. II. Garcia, Trixie, writer of foreword. III. Title.

ML419.G36A5 2015

782.42166092--dc23

[B]

2015026784

Contents

The conversations that went on in my childhood home were typically mind-blowing in one way or another. People may not know how brilliant my Dad was beyond his musical chops, but the fact is he was drawn to anything that would make him go "Wow!" He always seemed to be on a quest to learn everything he could about things that fascinated him. As a result, he was incredibly knowledgeable on a variety of subjects and always had some cool new thing to talk to people about. Beyond his love of music, Jerry's world was loaded with cosmic jokes, cartoon characters, campy horror flicks, weird coincidences and anything that seemed magical to him.

Trixie and Mountain Girl, 1975.

So it's a pleasure to be able to share with you now this rare window into both the fun-loving weirdness and more mysterious corners of my dad's inquisitive and insightful mind—from thoughts on Frankenstein to Weir, sometimes all at once!

Together with Marc Allan and Red Light Management, the Jerry Garcia Family is delighted to bring you these unpublished interviews, art, notes, and photos. The interview tapes were sourced from the Grateful Dead Archive at UC Santa Cruz, under Nicholas Meriwether's watchful eye. The Grateful Dead Archive is a wonderful thing, designed to steward the Grateful Dead's legacy through a scholastic point of view. The GD Archive has become part of a greater foundation of the Grateful Dead community and a place for many within the scene to share collections. Dennis McNally, who has, after so many years with the band, become a close family friend, was asked to help set the context of the interviews and lend his invaluable insights. Above all, it's Jerry's voice that we want and try to bring you with this book.

The art and handwritten notes are from my own personal collection and that of my mother's: Carolyn Garcia, Mountain Girl. We call this the Garcia Family Archive.

In the difficult years following the coma, my dad was in thrown into recovery mode. He had to relearn the guitar and when he or his fingers needed a break, he would draw. His skill in drawing from time spent as an art student helped him regain coordination and precision. Art became a new high for him. It was a much needed creative outlet for him, along with things like scuba diving, which he adored and which focused his mind.

Annabelle and Jerry celebrate Christmas at the Kesey Farm, 1982.

During this time an unending stream of art supplies of increasing complexity funneled into the house, mostly in the form of markers, pocket sketchbooks, and the occasional airbrush set. He would experiment with each new wave of supplies, and he was a talented visual artist—exploring materials, textures, techniques, and characters. Most of the art collected here comes from small spiral bound notebooks dating from 1985 through 1991.

Calligraphy was also a favorite exercise for his hands at this time. He filled many pages with nonsensical gibberish and whimsical rhymes, which he wrote in elaborate lettering. Funny-sounding, as well as funny-looking, words were one of his "things." I remember laughing with him one day over the silliness of the word "fjord." Just laughing and finding fun where he could, Jerry's delight in what he saw as the little absurdities of life was limitless.

I hope you enjoy taking this ride with him.

We miss him dearly.

– Trixie Garcia, 2015

Many photographers have been kind enough to share some very special
photos of Jerry for this book. Thank you to all the photographers who
continue to share their collections with us!

Jerry Garcia, 1969.

Very few things have been more fun and more stimulating for me than talking with Jerry Garcia. Both his playing and his life rested on dynamic interaction with other people; he listened. That love of, and indeed need for, interaction certainly applied to conversation, which, second to playing music, was probably his favorite activity. Jerry loved to rap—not just to talk, certainly not to hear himself go on, but to communicate, to exchange thoughts, to learn about other people. Even when his poor physical health caused him to be somewhat withdrawn and depressed toward the end of his life, he retained a profound curiosity about the lives of others. The celebrity interview, an opportunity for an artist to talk about himself and to pitch a current endeavor in as brief and efficient a manner as possible, was completely lost on Jerry. I once set him up for a *Rolling Stone* cover interview to promote a new record. The record barely got mentioned in the piece, and when I called up the interviewer to find out what had happened, he swore, "I tried to talk about the record. Jerry wanted to talk about his daughter (Keelin)."

Of course that's why people loved to talk with Jerry—he wanted to bond, to listen to you and learn your story, and to share his own. In the early days of the Garcia Band, Jerry would arrive at the Keystone in Berkeley and spend all afternoon running scales on his guitar, with a joint and a cup of coffee at hand. Occasionally he would tell his roadie and confidant Steve Parish, "Go get me someone weird." Steve would go out on the street, find someone reasonably odd—it was Berkeley, after all, so that was not terribly difficult—and bring them inside. Jerry would rap with the stranger all afternoon.

As Robert Hunter pointed out in a recent *Rolling Stone* interview, "To me, Jerry just had a really interesting mind, you know; he was just phenomenal, fun to talk to." Quite so. But there was more to the art of conversation for Jerry. He constantly repeated the phrase "you know." This wasn't some kind of verbal tic. He did it knowingly and purposefully, to emphasize equality. He assumed that you were on the same wavelength, that you and he were having a conversation. That this was not a lecture. That he was not a star and you were not a fan, but that you and he were partners in a verbal quest, and that he was glad you were there with him.

My first interview with Jerry took place in 1973, at the Gramercy Park Hotel in New York City after an Old & In the Way show at the Capitol Theatre in Passaic, New Jersey. I was a graduate student at the University of Massachusetts at Amherst working on a dissertation about Jack Kerouac. In the course of my research, I'd heard about a guy named Al Aronowitz, who was then the rock critic for the *New York Post*. This was the era when the Post was a left-leaning newspaper with great feature writers like Jimmy Breslin and Pete Hamill, as well as Al.

Al had written a ten-part series on the Beat Generation in 1960, probably the best journalism ever on the subject, and I'd called him to see if I could look at his files. He'd tried to write a book based on the series, but his inability to let go of the material, to simply finish the manuscript and turn it in, had blown his contract. When I showed up, it occurred to him that he could use my energy and academic credentials to get the Beat book published. As I studied the material and made suggestions, Al concluded that a new chapter on Neal Cassady, whom Al had interviewed in San Quentin (where he served two years for possession of two joints), would be just the thing—and that it would be essential to interview his friend and Neal's, the lead guitarist of the Grateful Dead, Jerry Garcia.

After seeing the show at the Capitol, we arrived at Jerry's suite and sat down with Jerry and his lady friend, whose name I can't recall. All I can tell you is that she was very beautiful. It was a long time ago, and in revisiting these tapes after more than four decades, I'm relieved that my questions, at least most of the time, weren't too terribly dumb. I remember that Jerry was gracious—he was that way throughout these interviews—and insightful. The interview confirmed his deep personal connection to the Beat Generation's literary and social movement of the '50s. It also revealed his profound respect for Neal Cassady, the man who created what Jerry described as a "Western model for getting high." As we were finishing up, Jerry brought out an excellent joint, and after we made our good-byes I sat in the shotgun seat of Al's car and floated back to his house in New Jersey, reflecting that if anybody in the world should have great weed, it was Jerry.

⟫⟫ ⟪⟪

Random House published *Desolate Angel*, my biography of Jack Kerouac, in 1979. By then I'd become a fairly serious Dead Head—I'd had all of two shows under my belt before that first talk with Jerry—and had come to see myriad connections between the Beats and the Grateful Dead, far beyond the obvious link that both Kerouac and the Dead had known Neal Cassady. Eventually, I decided that my next book would be volume two of a two-volume history of bohemia in America after World War II. The first volume, *Desolate Angel*, had covered the '40s and '50s through Kerouac's life, and the second volume would cover the '60s and '70s through the history of the Grateful Dead. I yearned to write about the Dead but had no effective way to approach them. I knew intuitively that if I simply contacted the band and announced my intention, I'd probably get a curt, "Take a number, kid." So I sent copies of *Desolate Angel* to Jerry and to Robert Hunter, Jerry's lyricist, at the Dead Head fan club mailing address, and waited.

That same year, as part of a subtle way to introduce myself to the band, I pitched the editor of the *San Francisco Chronicle's* Sunday magazine, *California Living*, on a piece about that special Dead Head ritual known as New Year's Eve, which that year would take place for the first time at the Oakland Auditorium (Winterland having closed the previous New Year's Eve). She liked the idea, and so early in 1980 I interviewed promoter Bill Graham about it—he at least had a public business phone number, which the Dead did not. As I was leaving his office, his assistant, Jan Simmons, told me I should talk to Eileen Law at the Dead office. Better still, she gave me Eileen's number.

The Grateful Dead's fifteenth anniversary had been in May of that same year. They planned to celebrate it with a series of fifteen shows at the Warfield Theatre in San Francisco, a brief stop in New Orleans, and then a substantial run ending on Halloween at New York City's Radio City Music Hall. There would be three sets each night, one acoustic and then the usual two electric ones. The Halloween show would be simulcast to movie theaters up and down the East Coast, and the broadcast would be hosted by the band's friends from *Saturday Night Live*, Al Franken and Tom Davis. They would fill up the time between sets on the broadcast with skits spoofing Jerry Lewis's telethons—their telethon would raise funds for Jerry (Garcia)'s Kids to be able to get to the next show. Early in the San Francisco run they auditioned Dead Heads to find one to portray Jerry's Kid for the Halloween show. Thanks to Eileen Law, I was one of those Dead Heads.

At the audition, we were asked to tell stories of being a Dead Head, but I soon mentioned the Kerouac book and got a warm response. Jerry had loved the book. Kerouac had played an important role in Jerry's life, particularly when he was a teenager. He served as an inspiring hero to Jerry when he was looking for validation as a young, free-thinking artist who would soon become a full-time musician. To paraphrase Jerry, *Desolate Angel* "confirmed his prejudices" about Kerouac. In December 1980, I met Grateful Dead staff members Rock Scully and Alan Trist at the Warfield Theatre (Dylan was playing his second run there, with Jerry, among many others, sitting in—it was Carlos Santana on the night I met with Rock and Alan), and they told me, "Jerry says, why don't you do us?", meaning a biography of the band. Damn. I'd dreamed about it for seven years at that point, and now what I'd silently willed into reality had dropped in my lap. And so I set to work, which of course included having many conversations with Jerry.

⟫⟫⟫ ⟪⟪⟪

11

This book is based on five interviews, totaling nearly nine hours, conducted with Jerry between 1973 and 1989. The first session took place in 1973 during the aforementioned sit-down with Al Aronowitz. The second and third sessions took place in 1984, after I'd become the band's publicist. (The receptionist had complained that nobody was dealing with the media, and Jerry had responded, "Get McNally to do it. He knows that shit.") We met in Jerry's downstairs studio apartment at 12 Hepburn Heights (Rock Scully and his family lived upstairs) in San Rafael, where we smoked a fair amount of dope, and had some great talks.

The fourth session happened in 1986, after Jerry was well on his way to recovering from his diabetic coma of earlier that year. Carolyn "Mountain Girl" (or "M.G.") Garcia was present for the session and joined in. By now, Jerry had moved into the upstairs level of the house at Hepburn Heights.

The final conversation is an interesting interview Jerry did in 1989 with a writer named Jeremy Alderson on the subject of LSD.

I know that at least two or three hours of tape that I made with Jerry in 1981 when I was getting started are missing—God knows how or where. I even remember the first question I asked—it was about the missing first joint of the middle finger on his right hand. When I sat down to review the tapes and consider how to organize them into some sort of coherent narrative for this book, I quickly realized that what we did have was an intimate window into his life before the Dead, a great deal about the early days of the Dead, and then quite a bit about the year 1969, a most interesting year in Grateful Dead history. So lining things up into a clear chronological sequence was fairly easy.

What should become quite clear is that these are not strictly interviews, but instead conversations, in which Jerry would divert a given topic to whatever subject came to mind. And I was more than happy to oblige this tendency. So we have philosophical asides on business management, politics, playing, and what he thought had been his coolest experiences as an appreciator of film, the visual arts, and above all, music. Since they did not fit directly into the chronology, I have separated them out into the sections we've named "Jerry on . . ."

When I finally sat down to write the band's biography, *A Long Strange Trip*, I was pained by all the fabulous material that had to be cut. These were the magical moments when Jerry would go into extensive detail on things like how his mind worked when he went into solos. It was stuff I'd never heard him talk about before— I'm reasonably sure I'd read every interview he'd ever given—and it was pure gold. I'm not sure how many musicians are able to so brilliantly articulate just exactly what it is that they do—I strongly suspect Jerry's close to unique. So it's a joy to share these moments with you now. Enjoy Jerry on Jerry—God knows I did.

– Dennis McNally, 2015

- **Carolyn Adams** was Jerry's second wife. A member of the Merry Pranksters, she earned the nickname "Mountain Girl" or more commonly "M.G." during that time. She was a coresident of 710 Ashbury Street, and had two children, Annabelle and Theresa ("Trixie") with Jerry. She also had a child with Ken Kesey, Sunshine, whom Jerry raised as his own.

- **Michelangelo Antonioni** was the Italian film director who made the classic *Blow-Up* and then brought in Jerry Garcia to record a portion of the music in *Zabriskie Point*.

- **Al Aronowitz** was a journalist with the *New York Post* who in the late '50s covered the Beat Generation. He later became the pop critic at the *Post* and thus became quite friendly with Jerry.

- *Big Brother and the Holding Company* was one of the primal rock bands of the San Francisco scene, and included Peter Albin, who'd been part of Garcia's folk scene on the Peninsula, and Janis Joplin, herself once a San Francisco folk musician.

- **Elmer Bischoff**, **Mark Rothko**, and **Clyfford Still** were prominent members at various times of the faculty of the California School of Fine Arts (now the San Francisco Art Institute). Their fame gave the school great standing.

- **Elvin Bishop** was a musician from Oklahoma who attended the University of Chicago and fell into the highly creative blues scene of the early 1960s there, joining the Butterfield Blues Band before moving to the Bay Area.

- **Lenny Bruce** was an American stand-up comedian who fell in love with jazz improvisation and shifted his material from jokes to a stream-of-consciousness spew of observations about almost everything. As much for his mocking of the Roman Catholic church as for scatological language, he became the subject of multiple obscenity arrests and eventually died of a drug overdose.

- **Herb Caen** was a legendary columnist (mostly) with the *San Francisco Chronicle* from the late 1930s to the turn of the century, and a daily part of the lives of many San Franciscans in that time, including Jerry's grandmother.

- **Bill "Kidd" Candelario** was a member of the Grateful Dead's road crew. He came into the band's orbit in 1968 at the Carousel Ballroom and never left. In later years he was primarily Phil Lesh's bass tech.

- **Neal Cassady**, known as "Dean Moriarity" in Jack Kerouac's *On the Road*, was a close friend of the Grateful Dead's and a spiritual mentor to Jerry Garcia.

- **Luria Castell** was the leader of a group of people, the Family Dog, who put on the first adult rock 'n' roll dances in San Francisco at the Longshoremen's Hall.

- **Ruth "Bobby" Clifford**, Jerry's mother. A trained nurse, she was interested in music; she had a good voice and exposed Jerry to opera.

- **Tillie Clifford**, grandmother. A free-thinker, labor union activist, and true San Franciscan. Jerry adored her.

- **The Crows**, an R&B street-corner doo-wop group from New York City, had a hit in 1953 with their first song, "Gee," which was the first R&B tune Jerry would recall hearing. He particularly liked the untrained street-corner quality to their vocals.

13

- **Joe** and **Jim Edmiston** were brothers and friends of Jerry. Union workers and a few years older than Jerry, they also loved to play bluegrass and were part of the "Thunder Mountain Tub Thumpers," which in Spring 1962 included Jerry on guitar, Robert Hunter on mandolin, and another friend, Ken Frankel, on fiddle.

- **Gary Foster** was a friend of Jerry's at the time Jerry was attending Analy High School in Sebastopol, north of San Francisco. His band, The Chords, was the first group Jerry played in.

- **Paul Foster** ran a folk club in San Jose called the Offstage and was later a Merry Prankster.

- **Clifford "Tiff" Garcia** was by four years Jerry's older brother. He introduced him to R&B music and EC Comics (*Tales from the Crypt*, for example), for which Jerry was always grateful. The nickname came from the very young Jerry's struggles to say his name.

- **Jose Garcia**, Jerry's father. A jazz musician (various reed instruments), he reportedly fell out with the Musician's Union and opened a bar called Joe's on the corner of 1st and Harrison Street.

- **Stephen Gaskin** was a spiritual leader in the Haight-Ashbury scene who later led a number of people in a move to "The Farm," a commune in Tennessee.

- **Allen Ginsberg**, American poet and author of "Howl," which he first read at the Six Gallery on Fillmore Street in San Francisco in October 1955. The manager of the gallery was Wally Hedrick.

- **Ken Goldfinger**, a drug dealer in the Bay Area who was a friend of the Grateful Dead's. His girlfriend, Nicki Rudolph, would later marry Rock Scully.

- **Bill Graham** was the business manager for the Mime Troupe who glimpsed the future of rock 'n' roll in the Bay Area and became the most important promoter of his generation.

- **Laird Grant** aka "Barney" was Garcia's best friend from junior high school and became one of the first Grateful Dead crew members.

- **Billy Grillo** was a member of the Grateful Dead road crew from the early 1980s to 1995. He was Bill Kreutzmann's drum tech.

- **David Grisman** was playing mandolin in the parking lot of a bluegrass park in Pennsylvania when he met Jerry; he went on to play on a Grateful Dead song and then to make many acoustic records with Jerry.

- **Emmett Grogan** was a member of the San Francisco Mime Troupe and part of a cohort of political/theatrical activists called the Diggers.

- **Mickey Hart** is a percussionist who joined the Grateful Dead in September 1967. He and drummer Bill Kreutzmann were known as the "Rhythm Devils."

- **Dan Healy** was a sound technician, designer, and mixer with the Grateful Dead from the 1960s to the 1990s. He came out of the world of radio, a "Gyro Gearloose" kid as he described himself, and brought an extraordinary flexibility and intelligence to what was then the fairly crude world of sound reinforcement.

- **Wally Hedrick** was a noted member of the "Funk Art" assemblage school of painting, and also taught at the California School of Fine Arts. He also played guitar and jazz banjo, and enjoyed playing music for his students. It was his playing of a Big Bill Broonzy record in Garcia's class that inspired Jerry to want to learn to play guitar. Wally also influenced Jerry morally, encouraging his bohemian tendencies to seek a life of art and spirit rather than money.

• **Chet Helms** was a San Francisco Lemar (Legalize Marijuana) activist who took over the name "Family Dog" and produced concerts at the Avalon Ballroom.

• **Peggy Hitchcock** was an heir to the Mellon fortune, a friend of Timothy Leary's who made him welcome at her family's Millbrook Estate, and a friend of Ron Rakow's.

• **Robert Hunter** was a fellow folk/bluegrass musician and one of Jerry's closest friends in the Palo Alto days; he would become Jerry's lyricist and a central pillar of the appeal of the Grateful Dead.

• **Erik Jacobsen** was the producer of The Lovin' Spoonful.

• **Dwight Johnson**, Jerry's seventh-grade teacher, was a second positive influence on the young Jerry, encouraging him to read seriously such authors as George Orwell and D. H. Lawrence, generally furthering what Miss Simon had started—a skeptical, iconoclastic, free-thinking young mind.

• **Paul Kantner** was a Bay Area folk musician who cofounded the Jefferson Airplane with Marty Balin.

• **Jorma Kaukonen** was the lead guitarist for the Jefferson Airplane and later for Hot Tuna.

• **Bill Keith** was a bluegrass banjo player of Garcia's generation who was the first "city billy" (i.e., non-Southerner) to play with The Master, Bill Monroe.

• **Alton Kelley** and **Stanley "Mouse" Miller** were among the earliest poster artists in the San Francisco scene. They would later do many album covers for the Grateful Dead.

• **Jack Kerouac**, American author, came to fame with the publication of *On the Road*, a jazz-influenced novel about two men and their friends, later known as the Beat Generation, wandering the American landscape. The book was published in September 1957 and had an immense effect on Jerry, who would read it around then while simultaneously attending the California School of Fine Arts on a part-time basis.

• **Ken Kesey** attended the University of Oregon and eventually was part of the creative writing program at Stanford that included Larry McMurtry, Wendell Berry, Robert Stone, and Ed McClanahan. After experiencing psychedelic drugs in a CIA-financed study ("Project MKUltra") being carried out at the VA hospital where he was also a night aide, he wrote *One Flew Over the Cuckoo's Nest,* and then *Sometimes a Great Notion*. Further experimenting with LSD in the company of his friends, the "Merry Pranksters," he, the Pranksters, and their young friends the Grateful Dead began to carry out a series of gatherings called "Acid Tests" which would have a massive social influence on the era of the 1960s—and after.

• **Deborah Koons** was a young woman Jerry met in the mid-1970s and formed a relationship with for about two years. It resumed in 1993, and they were married on February 14, 1994.

• **Eileen Law** was a Grateful Dead staff worker who became one of the fundamental connections between the band and the audience, the Dead Heads. Her demeanor and positive persona had a remarkable influence within the Dead in ways that were not obvious, but significant.

15

- **Katie Lee** was an American singer best-known for her work on *The Great Gildersleeve* radio program, one of Jerry's earliest musical memories. Coincidentally, she was the stepmother of a friend of Jerry's, Mickey Hart's one-time girlfriend, Jerilyn Brandelius.

- **Willy Legate** was another member of Jerry's circle in Palo Alto, an eccentric free-thinker who would later be the superintendent of the Grateful Dead's recording studio and its first tape archivist.

- **Phil Lesh** was an early friend of Jerry's in Palo Alto whom he would invite to join the Warlocks in 1965, just as it began.

- **Richard Loren** was a booking agent for Jefferson Airplane and the Doors who later became manager of the Grateful Dead. It was his vision that encouraged the Grateful Dead to play at the Great Pyramid of Gizeh in 1978.

- **Manasha Matheson** was Jerry's close companion from 1987 to 1992, and the mother of their daughter, Keelin.

- **Ed McClanahan** is a Kentucky-born writer who was a Wallace Stegner Fellow at Stanford University in 1962, which resulted in his falling into the circle of Ken Kesey. He would write various novels and autobiographical writing, but his "Grateful Dead I Have Known," in *Playboy* in 1972, is most directly relevant here.

- **Rosie McGee**, born Florence Nathan, was Phil Lesh's lover for some years in the 1960s; she was the first person around the Dead who was a photographer.

- **Scotty Moore** was a Chet Atkins–style fingerpicking guitarist with a variation—he used a thumbpick—and came to fame after Sam

Phillips of Sun Records put Scotty and Bill Black together with Elvis Presley.

- **David Nelson** was a young friend of Jerry's who played guitar in many of Jerry's old-time and bluegrass bands and later joined him with the New Riders of the Purple Sage.

- **Steve Parish** met the Grateful Dead road crew in 1969 at a Dead show in Flushing, New York, his hometown. He soon moved to San Francisco and became a full-time crewmember in 1970. In 1977 he became Jerry's guitar tech, and eventually the manager of the Jerry Garcia Band. He would later write a memoir, *Home Before Daylight*.

- **Ms. B. Parker**, Chief Economic Officer; Bonnie Parker was the Dead's chief financial person from 1970 to 1987.

- **Charlie Parker** was an alto saxophonist who introduced great complexity into both harmonic and rhythmic components of jazz in the 1940s, leading to a music called "bebop," or "bop" for short.

- **Wilfried "Sätty" Podriech** was a San Francisco artist and printmaker in the 1960s with many interests in the occult.

- **Sparky Raizene** was a Grateful Dead crewmember in the 1970s.

- **Ron Rakow** was a former stock trader who became president of Grateful Dead Records and left under a cloud of scandal.

- **Hugh "Wavy Gravy" Romney** was a Beat poet and later friend and associate of the Merry Pranksters. He would remain a close friend of the Dead's.

- **Sandy Rothman** was a member of various Garcia folk bands; he and Jerry traveled to the South and Midwest on a bluegrass pilgrimage in 1964.

- **Sara Ruppenthal** was Jerry's first wife. They married in 1963 and had a daughter, Heather.

- **Merl Saunders** was a San Francisco jazz organ player; in the 1970s he formed a band with Garcia that would be quite popular.

- **John Sebastian** is a musician whose musical evolution paralleled Jerry's; he began as a folkie, joined the Even Dozen Jug Band, and then responded to Beatlemania by organizing the folk-rock The Lovin' Spoonful.

- **Rock Scully** and **Danny Rifkin** were the Grateful Dead's first comanagers.

- **Lawrence "Ram Rod" Shurtliff** earned his nickname as a member of the Merry Pranksters; while in Mexico, he jokingly proclaimed himself "Ramon Rodriguez Rodriguez," their guide. An Oregon farm boy, he was a man of great probity and ethical judgment, so trusted by the band that he would become the company president.

- **Miss Simon**, Jerry's third-grade teacher, was arty, bohemian, and of great importance to Jerry in encouraging his artistic side with projects; the result was his early identity as an artist and a free-thinker who was "different," and glad of it.

- **Paul Speegle** was a friend of Jerry's who died in a car accident on February 20, 1961. Garcia was in the accident as well but suffered only minor injuries. The event had a significant effect on him.

- **Ron Stevenson** was a friend of Garcia's from the U.S. Army. It was Garcia's attempt to counsel him away from suicide that caused Jerry to miss several reporting times and would lead to Jerry's general discharge. Ron also taught Jerry some rudiments of fingerpicking acoustic guitar.

- **Owsley Stanley**, commonly called "Bear," was legendary for making extremely high-quality LSD; he was also the Grateful Dead's early sound man.

- **Scotty Stoneman** was a bluegrass fiddler. A member of the Kentucky Colonels, he deeply impressed Garcia, who called him "the Charlie Parker of bluegrass" for his extraordinary playing.

- **Sue Swanson**, **Connie Bonner**, and **Bob Matthews** were high school friends of Bob Weir and are the first Dead Heads.

- **Eric Thompson** was a Bay Area guitarist and friend of Garcia's who went to New York and played with the East Coast pickers.

- **Alan Trist** was a British student on a year's holiday between "high school" and college who became part of Jerry's circle in Palo Alto. A few years later in 1970 he joined the Grateful Dead's staff as the manager of Ice-Nine, the band's music publishing firm.

- **Jacques Valle** is a computer scientist and astronomer credited with doing important work in mapping Mars for NASA and developing the precursor to the Internet, ARPANET. He is, with the astronomer Allen Hynek, among the more credible researchers on the subject of Unidentified Flying Objects ("UFOs"), a subject of great interest to Jerry.

- **Troy Weidenheiner** was a Palo Alto musician whose rock band the Zodiacs, occasionally had a substitute bass player named Jerry Garcia.

- **Bob Weir** was a Palo Alto high school student and musician when he met Jerry on December 31, 1963. He joined with him on "Mother McCree's Uptown Jug Champions," then the Warlocks, and then the Grateful Dead.

17

1

The Days Before the
Days Between

San Francisco is not like other places. The poet Kenneth Rexroth observed that every other city in America had come into existence for reasons connected to the Protestant work ethic—in other words, for reasons of commerce. But San Francisco became a city because a bunch of crazed gold-seekers decided to uproot themselves from their homes and risk everything to chase dreams of wealth. They came not only from the East Coast of the United States but also from South America (Chile in particular) and China. And even when they settled down and built an opera house and developed a conventionally corrupt city government, they retained a streak of individuality that cherished the eccentric, the goofy, and the bizarre—freedom, in fact—in ways that (excepting perhaps New Orleans) no other American city could claim. Jerry was a true San Franciscan.

Jerry and his father Joe and mother Ruth, 1942.

He talks here about his love affair with the city and about growing up Roman Catholic, which means of course that he talks about guilt and sexuality. Most Dead Heads know that the Garcia name came not from south of the U.S. border but from Spain (he was Irish and Swedish on his mother's side), but, in fact, ethnicity meant very little to him. The central person in Jerry's life throughout his childhood was his maternal grandmother, Tillie Clifford, who largely raised him and was a special woman. Also a true heir to San Francisco, she was a socialist, a free love advocate (at least for herself!), and a union activist.

He then touches on his earliest musical influences—the folk songs he first heard, the Grand Ole Opry (which may be hard to connect with San Francisco, but shows the power of a burgeoning radio network), his mother's love for opera, and, finally, television, which remained an automatic element in his life—the tube was permanently if silently on at home and on the road. Turning it on as soon as he arrived in a hotel room was as much a part of entering the room as setting down his suitcase.

 **Start of Interview**

JERRY: San Francisco—for me, San Francisco was something I was always conscious of. You know what I mean? I don't know how kids normally take the place they grew up, but for me, San Francisco was a magic place. I mean, I used to go out to Sutro's and places like that and just breathe in the reality of it. You know what I mean? I just loved those places. I went there from the time I could get on a fuckin' Muni bus, you know, or a streetcar. From the moment I could get on those damn things, and cop a dime somewhere to do it, I was all over that city. That's the neat thing about San Francisco—it's a pocket city.

DENNIS: Oh, it's the greatest.

JERRY: You can get anywhere, you know? And God, I don't remember ever feeling threatened or even slightly, you know, intimidated by any part of the city or anything. I walked around everywhere. I turned over every rock, you know, at least a couple of times. I don't remember being scared of anything. I just had nothing but great fun.

DENNIS: Were you conscious that it was different from the rest of America or were you—

JERRY: I didn't know what the rest of America was like. For me, I didn't know. . . . I didn't have that sophisticated of a notion of other places really at all.

DENNIS: As a little kid, how old were you when you stopped going to mass? One, if you did go to mass or church—

JERRY: I stopped going to mass when we moved down the peninsula because before that when I lived in San Francisco, I lived a block from Corpus Christi [Church]. You know? I just had to go around the corner and I was there. And I went because I don't think I had the imagination to do anything else, really. I mean, I don't think it would have occurred to me, because I was asthmatic and everything. It would have been great trouble to run away or to run—to go someplace else.

21

"San Francisco was something I was always conscious of . . .
For me, San Francisco was a magic place."

Clockwise from upper left: Jerry and Joe, c. 1947. Jerry at church, c. 1951. Baptism (from the left: Tillie Clifford [Jerry's grandmother], Joe, Jerry, Tiff, and family friends), c. 1942. Tiff and Jerry, c. 1947. Baby Jerry, 1942. Jerry and Santa, c. 1947. Jerry, Tiff, and Cousin Diane, c. 1951.

DENNIS: Cuts down your options.

JERRY: I don't think I would have thought of it. When we moved down the peninsula and the Catholic church was quite a long way away, that's when I started really lapsing out. So I made my First Communion, but I wasn't ever confirmed. That's when I lopped off.

DENNIS: About twelve.

JERRY: About the year you can get confirmed, that's when I stopped going.

DENNIS: That's when you were eleven, which is when you moved down to Menlo?

JERRY: Yeah.

24

California Mission.
Gouache on paper.

DENNIS: I've never known a Roman Catholic girl who didn't have problems with sex. How much was growing up in the Roman Catholic church [an influence on you, as it was on your hero Jack Kerouac]?

JERRY: Always weird for me. Yeah, because of the . . . just the hang-up between what I would describe as love and sex. You know? Those were the things that always hung me up, but I—I had a hard time being just loose, sexually, really. It was hard for me to just fuck somebody. I never enjoyed that.

DENNIS: Mm-hmm.

JERRY: I was never very good at it. I really had to love somebody to have a good sexual relationship with them. At least for a while.

DENNIS: Yeah, I was going to say, on the other hand I've heard enough stories about—

JERRY: Then it stopped mattering. That part of it never—the sexual part of it never really hung me up that seriously, at least, that I'm conscious of, insofar as that sex for me has never been a real leading thing in my life. Except for when it really runs you around crazy, like when you're around fourteen or so. You know?

DENNIS: Right.

JERRY: You know, when you're really nuts.

DENNIS: Permanent chemical overdose.

JERRY: Right.

DENNIS: I was thinking of it more as generalized guilt and more in the sense of—

JERRY: For me it tended to be generalized guilt, which probably was sexual in nature. I mean, at root, you know . . . See, Catholicism for me never reached me sexually. I don't remember ever being told anything about the existence of sex, even, in Catholicism. For me, Catholicism was much more a matter of the invisible world. It bent me much more in that . . . the Justin Green way, you know what I mean? Did you ever read *Binky Brown Meets the Holy Virgin Mary*? [A very funny satirical, autobiographical comic book about growing up Roman Catholic.]

DENNIS: No, but—

JERRY: You've got to pick it up, by Justin Green. It's the ultimate in the neurotic Catholic rundown. Really. It's got the whole story in there. You've got to read it. It's one of the best exposés of the Catholic kid. You know? And the way you're warped when you're a Catholic kid. I mean, you've got to read it. I'll go through it with you and show you, "Now, this is me, and this is not. This is me." You know what I mean?

DENNIS: Okay. Yeah.

JERRY: Because it's that right on.

DENNIS: Great. Okay.

JERRY: It's so right on. It was the kind of stuff I'd go, "Yeah. Oh, fuck." It warped me much more in the world of the invisible. You know what I mean? Which is much stranger. I mean, the world of hell. I was never a deep Catholic. I never went to Catholic school, you know. I never was at catechism enough to get a picture of what it was they were trying to tell me about. For me, the most real thing about Catholicism was my presence in the church and the awesome sense that the church could fill you with just the reality of it and the rumbling of the Latin mass, the sensual—

DENNIS: The theater.

JERRY: The theater got to me much more than any ideas. You know what I mean? So I never developed a sense of morality of the church. I wasn't exposed to it. Nobody in my family went to church. Well, I was the kind of Catholic kid where my grandmother would give me a quarter, you know, to put in the collection plate, and that was church.

DENNIS: Did you have any particular sense of ethnicity of yourself?

JERRY: Not really. My mother used to tell me the story about how when she—when my father first took her to meet his family, and she said to my grandfather when he first met her, "Well, hello, Mr. Garcia, you know I just love Mexican food." And so the next time she went down there, my grandfather had gotten together, I guess had bought a tortilla and some hamburgers and it was just like, you know, the patty of hamburger with a tortilla wrapped around it. And it was like this joke, and she was totally embarrassed. She didn't realize that Spanish, the Spanish culture, is different than Mexicans', than the Mexican culture, and that was like her big faux pas, you know? And she used to tell me about that as sort of an illustrative thing.

Now, for me, the hit that I got from my Spanish relatives—my Spanish relatives were always very, very straight. To give you an inclination, my Spanish relatives were the kind of people that when my mother died, they wouldn't let my mother be buried next to my father because she'd remarried after he died. That's an indication of how straight they are.

DENNIS: Right.

JERRY: You know? I mean, that's the kind of people they are. And . . . also, my cousins whose last names were Garcia changed their last names to anglicize their last names. I have a cousin who's an optometrist or something like that, so that he wouldn't get Mexican customers, you know, thinking that he was Mexican. Like that. You know? They were really straight and they're very conscious of being Spanish rather than Mexican, you know? And they also have that light Spanish coloring. My dark coloring comes from the Irish side of the family, not from the Spanish side. My Spanish relatives are all sallow complected, kind of brown, reddish-brown hair, and they have that look. You know? So for me [that was] the idea of being Spanish, really, apart from the fact that my grandparents on my father's side spoke Spanish, I think exclusively, and that I learned to speak, really, Spanish speaking to them. But I don't remember when I learned it or how I learned it. I didn't really remember it until I went to Spain. When we went to Spain [the Dead played the Sports Palace in Barcelona on October 19, 1981], all of a sudden, there were people who spoke to me with the same accent as my grandparents had. And all of a sudden, it was as though they were speaking English. All of a sudden, I could understand them.

DENNIS: Even though—

JERRY: I couldn't understand the others, but I could understand them—

27

DENNIS: If some Cuban guy walked up to you right now, you would be going—

JERRY: No way. And Mexican on the radio I can't pick up either, but these people I could understand them, you know, pretty well.

DENNIS: Wow, that's wild.

JERRY: Really. It was . . .what? A flash. You know? It reverberated.

DENNIS: "I just learned the language! Painlessly!"

JERRY: Right. And it completely blew my mind. You know?

DENNIS: I'll bet.

JERRY: Yeah, because I didn't remember, don't remember, learning it and don't remember thinking of myself as knowing Spanish. You know? I even took Spanish in high school. You know? And then this is something that goes so far back, I don't even remember where it comes from. So that was a real funny experience for me. And it was just weird. you know? I couldn't understand every bit of it, but most of it I could understand. You know? And it was so funny how it suddenly came across and kind of jumped tracks. It was a weird experience. Now I know what that's like.

DENNIS: Uh huh.

JERRY: I didn't think I knew what that was like, but I do. The bilingual thing.

DENNIS: The point is, with you, it's all ear.

JERRY: Yeah.

DENNIS: And when that accent—

JERRY: Right.

DENNIS: It rang some change, could get through.

JERRY: That's right. It was exactly that. I remember, because all of a sudden . . . It was one of those things, you know how you remember something, like when you get a smell, you know, and you get a full-impact sensorial remembrance of something, and all of a sudden the whole moment comes back? Well, that was the experience that came back when I heard that language, and it rang it right in, just the way one of those olfactory things does. It was far out. It blew my mind. It was something I didn't know about myself. That was just a couple of years ago.

DENNIS: Yeah. Right.

JERRY: So there was that, but I never thought of that as ethnicity. You know what I mean? As far as I knew, there were no . . . I didn't know there were different kinds of people, really, until I moved down the peninsula and first started hearing about Jews or something like that, and I knew people who were, who were joining something called Job's Daughters and DeMolay and all that stuff.

DENNIS: Right. And you couldn't be Catholic.

JERRY: And all of a sudden I was like, what? People, they don't like Catholics? I don't understand it. Those things, they were all very alien to me because my grandmother was so unselfconsciously universal. I don't remember her ever saying anything about anybody—I don't remember her ever differentiating any way about anybody. You know?

DENNIS: God knows her work in that union was the ultimate multiracial—

JERRY: Right. Absolutely.

DENNIS: Had to be.

JERRY: Right.

DENNIS: That's the thing. You've got this very straight conservative element in your past and then, you know, you've got your kick-ass grandma.

JERRY: Right.

> "And all of a sudden I was like, what? People, they don't like Catholics? I don't understand it. Those things, they were all very alien to me because my grandmother was so unselfconsciously universal."

Flamenco Dancer.
Pen and ink on paper.

DENNIS: With a hard-core social—

JERRY: Luckily my grandmother raised me.

DENNIS: Exactly.

JERRY: I think she must have been a real socialist. I don't know, but she must have been pretty far out there.

But I remember I was really taken with her. I mean, I thought she was just great, you know, and I always did. I always admired her a lot, and my mom, too. My mom did something difficult, too. I remember my grandmother, she used to tell how hard it was getting my grandfather to go for her to go to school, you know, to go to nurses' school and become a career person.

DENNIS: Mm-hmm.

JERRY: You know? She said that was like pulling teeth. But she was strong, too. They were strong. I mean, I never thought of it. You know? I didn't necessarily think about it when I was growing up, and there it was.

DENNIS: You and Phil have these very interesting grandmothers, you know, super-neat female role models—

JERRY: Far out.

DENNIS: —in your lives. You know, Phil's grandma turned him on to music, you know?

JERRY: Oh, I didn't know Phil's grandma was the one that turned him on. That's great.

DENNIS: When he was four, she caught him listening at a doorway and he remembers, as you would expect Phil to remember, who was playing and what they—

JERRY: Right.

DENNIS: I think it was Brahms's First Symphony—

JERRY: Right. I know. I had him tell me about it before.

Old-time Couple.
Pen and ink on paper.

DENNIS: And she saw him interested, and she came in and dragged him in and sat him in front the radio, and he fell down the rabbit hole and has been Phil Lesh ever since.

JERRY: Right. Out of sight, right, right.

DENNIS: Just amazing stuff.

JERRY: That was the other thing. My mom was into music, too, which she sang. Apparently, she was pretty into it when she was in school and she was, like, into operettas and that as a singer, and she played a little piano, and she was an opera buff, too, an opera nut, too. I mean, she was big on it. I grew up with ears full of opera all the time.

DENNIS: No shit.

JERRY: Yeah, she was big on classical music and big on opera. Big fan of all kinds of— I remember all kinds of names from those days, and she took me to the opera once in a while. And she was a big fan of Leonard Warren and Risë Stevens and the opera singers who were famous in those days, in the forties . . . Yeah. I was always hearing her, and would sing snatches of arias. She had a pretty good soprano voice and she played a little "Moonlight Sonata" on the piano and enjoyed it. She was a big music buff, and I'm sure that was one of the reasons she got on with my old man.

》》》 《《《

DENNIS: Couple of things that people have told me. One was that you had remarked that you listened to a lady named Katie Lee on *The Great Gildersleeve* radio show?

JERRY: Yeah.

DENNIS: That would be true?

JERRY: Yes. Jerilyn's mother. [Jerilyn Brandelius is a member of the extended Grateful Dead family, who was once Mickey Hart's partner. Katie Lee was her stepmother.]

DENNIS: Oh, okay. I know Jerilyn told me, but I didn't realize that was her mother.

JERRY: Yeah. Jerilyn's stepmother or mother-in-law, mother something. Yeah, Jerilyn's mom. Yeah.

DENNIS: Oh. Okay. That's why she told me, obviously.

JERRY: I remember that from when I was a little kid. I mean, a little, little kid. You know?

DENNIS: At that point, you know, what were your connections with sort of the outside world, as it were? Radio, obviously. I mean, you were a little kid before television.

JERRY: Jeez, I don't remember. I mean, I remember more the effect. There was something about that that was so . . . It was very romantic to me even though I was just a little kid. Something about her voice. You know? And this was before— I mean, I didn't know anything about music then. I wasn't aware of styles, or . . . I wasn't aware there was such a thing as country music. This was when I was a little kid. And for me, all music was just undifferentiated stuff that came out of the radio. But I remember that because it was the thing of the beautiful, the unaccompanied female voice. You know? Seeing these folk musics—it was the purity of it that got to me, and the pure melodic thing of it that just got right to me. I don't know, something about it that said something to my soul. You know? I couldn't say what it was. It was a totally emotional thing.

DENNIS: Uh huh.

JERRY: And I don't know if I'd recognize it now or anything. I don't remember the context or anything. I just remember that . . . You know? I didn't really remember this at all in my conscious mind until I read on the back of one of Jerilyn's mom's records that she had worked with the Great Gildersleeve on the radio and then it, *bong*, it flashed me back and it was so far out. I remembered myself as a little kid in my room, me and my brother, listening to the radio, you know, at night . . . And the thing about radio is that you spun the worlds of radio in your head. You know? And so radio drama had that wonderful thing of the mental world, and—

DENNIS: Much more creative.

JERRY: Must have been before '48.

DENNIS: Uh huh.

JERRY: Or right around '48.

DENNIS: You think that might have been your first heavy connection with a musical—

JERRY: No. That wasn't the first, but it was one of them. The very first one was when I must have been three or four or something like that, and there was a record of some tune like, I think it was "The Girl I Left Behind." Another little folk song, a little marching song or something like that. And a windup phonograph that my grandparents had up in their country place. There was no electricity, just a windup phonograph with the little needles and a few, [a] handful of old records, mostly the one-sided kind, the really old—

DENNIS: Jesus.
JERRY: I mean, you know this is, like, old dusty shit.

DENNIS: Uh huh.
JERRY: Nobody listened to this or even looked at it but me. And there was this one record, and I put it on and I'd play it and I'd play it, and I'd wind up the thing and play it over and over again. I played it for hours on end. I don't know what it was about it, but I remember doing that and I remember there being something about the song, something about the music. It was like scratching an itch. There was also . . . It was, like, "Sweet Betsy from Pike," one of those American folk songs. You know? And there was just something about it that I had to hear a million times. I mean, I could have heard it a gazillion times and I still would want to hear it one more time. I mean, I literally wore those records flat. I don't know why. It was like a compulsion, almost. It was like . . . Nobody showed me how to do it. Nobody said, "Now, listen to that," or nothing like that. It was something I discovered myself. And I mean, everybody was, "Turn that damn thing off. Take that outside and play." You know what I mean?

DENNIS: Right.
JERRY: They were so sick of listening to it. I just played it over and over and over again. I couldn't have been more than four, you know, three or four, maybe.

DENNIS: Great. Somebody quoted you once as saying that your grandma listened to *The Grand Ole Opry*.
JERRY: Right.

DENNIS: You could get it in San Francisco?

35

JERRY: Oh, sure. Because it was network. It was everywhere. On Saturday night, *The Grand Ole Opry* was on at least an hour everywhere. It didn't run like it did on WSM, all night long.

DENNIS: It did?

JERRY: Oh, yeah. It probably still does, WSM. It runs in half-hour packets, and each one is fronted by a different artist, but the whole thing is *The Grand Ole Opry*. It's *The Grand Old Opry* beginning to end. But the network version of it was like an hour, I think. And, you know, there would be all the different acts. I remember listening. And my grandmother loved it. She loved that, and she loved Hawaiian music.

〉〉〉 〈〈〈

DENNIS: I said, "Listen, Garcia feels that any room with room service and an electric guitar in it is fully furnished."

JERRY: Yeah, that's home to me. Yeah, shit. A TV, too.

DENNIS: And a TV, that's right.

JERRY: For me, a TV is like wallpaper. I don't actually watch it that much.

DENNIS: It's just there.

JERRY: Yeah, having it going is kind of like an electronic fireplace or something. I'm one of the first of the kids from the TV age, you know. I took to that sucker immediately, you know? When that Hoffman came in the front door.

DENNIS: Was it? Was it a Hoffman?

JERRY: I think so. I think it was our family's first. My grandmother had the first TV on the block.

DENNIS: We didn't get one until, like, the middle fifties.

JERRY: Oh, yeah, we got ours in '49.

DENNIS: Who did you grab on to? Uncle Miltie?

JERRY: Yeah, sure, Uncle Miltie. *Time for Beany* was one of the important things for me. The old *Beany*, the puppet show, that was done by—get this—it was done by—

DENNIS: Bob Clampett and Stan Freberg.

JERRY: That's right, yeah, they did *Time for Beany*, which was a black-and-white puppet show at that time. It's one of the very earliest TV experiences that I remember. And later on, Jackie Gleason in that era, you know, and *The Toast of the Town* [aka *The Ed Sullivan Show*], Sid Caesar and Imogene Coca and all that stuff. I was there from the very beginning of TV.

DENNIS: Right.

JERRY: It was great. Man, I loved early TV. It was so formless, so straight. There was one country and western program in the Bay Area. [*Hayride*, on KGO, in 1950] One live country [show, hosted by]—Dude Martin, and he featured—the guy he featured was Rusty Draper, who was the guy that made a popular single record of "Freight Train."

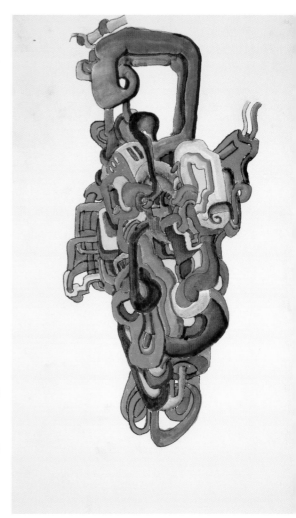

Magenta Heart.
Pen and colored ink on paper.

DENNIS: Okay.

JERRY: Rusty Draper, he was the finger-picking guitar player.

Jerry on Film

Jerry loved the movies. He loved to watch them, write them, direct them, and play in them. He directed *The Grateful Dead Movie*, codirected *So Far*, and cowrote a script for a film adaptation of Kurt Vonnegut's *The Sirens of Titan* with his friend Tom Davis, although they couldn't get it made. As far back as Palo Alto in the early '60s, when his wife, Sara, was taking film classes at Stanford, he borrowed an eight-millimeter camera from a friend and with the aid of various cohorts, Robert Hunter and Ron "Pigpen" McKernan among them, he even made some comic short movies.

He loved talking about them, too. In the last year of his life, clearly not himself and plagued by diabetes (which he didn't treat properly), his mood swings made him somewhat silent and withdrawn. I didn't ask him to do interviews—there was no urgent need for them, and he clearly didn't want to be bugged. But one day I got a call from a producer for the AMC program *The Movie That Changed My Life*, and immediately thought, here was something he'd be interested in. And indeed he was.

A day or two later he was at the Warfield for a Jerry Garcia Band show, and I stopped by the dressing room and mentioned the invitation. Bursting with enthusiasm, he was so pleased with the idea that he instantly launched into the interview. The movie that had changed Jerry's life had been *Abbott and Costello Meet Frankenstein*. Not exactly *Citizen Kane*, but it lit the cinema fuse for Jerry. The movie came out in 1948, when he was six, and it imprinted itself on his mind so firmly that he was able to describe to me the pattern of the upholstery on the seat in front of him in the theater, which was where his eyes went when things got too scary on the screen. He went on to link the three monsters in the film (Frankenstein was accompanied by Dracula and the Wolf Man) with the three members of World War II's Axis (Germany, Italy, and Japan) and talk about Lon Chaney Jr.'s makeup techniques, and then went into the horror genre in general, including Stephen King and Clive Barker. You can find this interview on YouTube, and it's hilarious.

Here, he talks about somewhat more sophisticated movies.

Feather, Alien, Picard, Frankenstein.
Mixed media on paper.

| Start of Interview

DENNIS: You were talking about *La Dolce Vita* [a 1960 comedy/drama by Federico Fellini about a journalist torn between different possible lives in post–World War II Rome]. Do you remember any other movies—like *Blow-Up*—that approached—had an impact? [*Blow-Up* was an important film starring David Hemmings and Vanessa Redgrave directed by Michelangelo Antonioni that captured the era of mid-sixties London and explored photography, identity, and the world of the observer and the observed.]

JERRY: There were certain oddities. I can't think of any that were, like, big deals. The Beatles ones were.

DENNIS: Yeah. Different ones.

JERRY: There was always stuff that had some kind of effect. You know? You ever see *Last Year at Marienbad*? [An enigmatic, dreamlike film by Alain Resnais released in 1961. It concerns ambiguous characters in a confusing environment.]

DENNIS: No.

JERRY: Strange movie. It's one of the new wave directors. I can't remember which one it is, but it's a strange . . . it's a very lovely movie. It's in some kind of incredibly ornate European spa, and these people are constantly . . . they're all kind of wooden, and there is, like, a play within the movie, and there are all these weird, shifting things going on, and lots of shots of balustrades, balconies, and flying buttresses and incredible-looking, kind of baroque, gothic, nightmare architecture, you know, this incredible ornate European shit. I can't even begin to describe what this place is like. And the characters move kind of woodenly through it and it's kind of dreamlike and there is this kind of stuff happening where one character starts a line and another character in another scene finishes it—dreamy, strange, yeah . . .

And in it there's these people who play this game with matchsticks. It's this thing of rows where you take so many matches out in each row and you end up leaving—the point is you're supposed to leave one match, but it's one of those things where unless you know how to do it, you lose every time or you win every time. It was one of those kinda things. Anyway, that was one of those kinds of movies. But this is not stuff that went out to society at large or even to a scene. It was, like, a handful of people.

DENNIS: Right. Oh, yeah.
JERRY: It was those kinds of things that—

DENNIS: Sara was doing the film courses and all that—
JERRY: Yeah, well . . .

DENNIS: —you fooling around with that camera.
JERRY: I mean, for me, a lot of movies—I'm a movie kid. You know? And I'm a movie buff to boot. Shit, there are all kinds of movies. Certainly, I'm a sucker for movies. If a movie isn't really awful, I can pretty much watch it and like it, unless there's something really wrong with it.

Dracula in Black.
Mixed media on paper.

41

DENNIS: Since I began working for the band, in particular, and even before that, I spent so many nights a year out, and then in particular with the book, it's like—it's very hard to drag me out of the house to a movie just because, you know, I'd rather sit and stare at Mac.
JERRY: Right. But—yeah, that's true. And it's disappointing to not see a good movie.

DENNIS: I did see one good one recently. The guy at Channel 7 has some kind of deal with all the film companies, and they get free tickets by the buckets and he sends some to me, and we went and saw . . . The only Stephen King book I ever read was [*Different Seasons*] and there is one where the boys—

JERRY: Find the body.

DENNIS: Find the body.

JERRY: Great movie. *Stand by Me*.

⟫⟫⟫ ⟪⟪⟪

JERRY: Stephen King has a real touch with characters. I read all his books. I like horror stories. Stephen King writes well.

DENNIS: If you like horror movies, I'll recommend it to you. I do not like horror movies. I spent most of the movie [referring to *The Fly*], I swear to God, Susana and I were holding, you know, doing the—

JERRY: I gotcha.

DENNIS: Peeking through [our fingers, barely able to watch at all]. But, oh, man, so brilliant. *The Fly*.

JERRY: *The Fly*. [David] Cronenberg is an excellent moviemaker.

DENNIS: Jeff Goldblum deserves an Academy Award for his performance. I swear, it's a great physical performance of this guy. Have you seen it?

JERRY: I haven't seen it.

DENNIS: Oh, goddamn. Go see it. I still get the cold shakes from it.

JERRY: Yeah.

DENNIS: Because the lighting, the cinematography itself, the special effects, and the acting are—

JERRY: This guy Cronenberg has a real knack for a memorable image. You know? He made a movie called *Scanners*, which is not a very good movie, but it's got one scene where the guy's head blows up. It's like, whoa. And he also made an amazing weird movie called *Videodrome*.

DENNIS: Yeah. [Grateful Dead crew member Bill] Candelario loves that movie.

JERRY: It's a very, very weird movie, but Cronenberg's sense of the break in reality and his fascination with nature—in a weird way.

DENNIS: Well, it's funny because, of course, I saw the original [*The Fly*, 1958], and all I remember—because I don't have a great visual memory, at least for movies, mostly, unless they're really important—but all I remember, of course, is that epic—

JERRY: "Help me."

DENNIS: —last scene. "Help me. Help me." Who can forget?

JERRY: That's a real icon.

DENNIS: Exactly. The head and the body, the fly, "Help me." You can't forget that.

JERRY: No, no.

DENNIS: This is much more horrific. I mean, a lot of it is very horrific because . . . Well, I won't blow the plot for you.

JERRY: I love that shit.

DENNIS: You'll love it.

JERRY: Yeah, great.

DENNIS: I'm not necessarily a great movie critic, but I think it's brilliantly done. I was, like, spooked almost from the time I started it, and—

JERRY: I gotta go see it. My kids loved it. Yeah, they loved it.

DENNIS: It's wild. It's wild. God, it was really funny. And I'm just not a—

JERRY: Jeez, I saw a good little movie that M. G. [Jerry's wife, Carolyn Adams "Mountain Girl" or M. G. Garcia] turned me on to. We rented the videotape of it. It's called *Dream*—what is it? *Dream Girl*? *Dream Child*? [*Dreamchild*, 1985.] Something like— Anyway, it's about Alice, of Alice in Wonderland. You know, the real Alice. And it's a movie about when she's in her eighties and she comes to New York.

Sweet ghoul.
Mixed media on paper.

DENNIS: I remember a rave review of that.

JERRY: It's a wonderful movie. What a wonderful movie. It's a great movie to rent and look at it at home.

It goes back to when Alice was little in Victorian England with Reverend Dodgson telling her stories with his terrible stammer, you know, and his obvious love for [her]— it's very, very tender. You know? It's handled so exquisitely. You know? And then here's Alice, eighty years old, a lady who's been through her life and, you know, she is just marvelous. The actress who plays her is absolutely marvelous, and it's a period piece, thirties, you know, New York City, and here she is, trying to explain this relationship or trying to explain something of how it wasn't her, it was the reverend, and she was mean to him when she was little, you know, and all this stuff, you know? Then it goes directly into *Alice in Wonderland* itself. The characters are done by Jim Henson [Henson's Creature Shop built the puppets for the dream sequences], and they're, like, slightly horrible. They're not really funny, you know what I mean? It's . . . all of a sudden, you're at the Mad Tea Party. Only the March Hare is kind of evil, and the Mad Hatter is mean, and Alice is old Alice.

DENNIS: Oh, it's the old—

JERRY: Right. The old Alice there. It's sort of drifting through her mind. You know? And it's a wonderful movie. It really is.

>>> <<<

[**Finally, one of Jerry's favorite subjects was UFOs, so *Close Encounters of the Third Kind* was pretty well made for him.**]

JERRY: I was glad that somebody was brave enough to make a movie about that weird—I always applaud the weirdness in human life. You know what I mean? I mean, such as it appears. That's the stuff that's fun to look out for because, what the fuck? You know? We've already burned out the normal shit.

DENNIS: Exactly.

JERRY: Right, so, you know, so it's the strange, the dark alleys that interest me, and that whole experience. I'm not talking about contact with the extraterrestrials and all that part of the movie, the fantasy part of the movie, but the part of the movie that deals with that tremendous difficulty anybody who's had a truly weird experience has getting back to regular life, if they ever get back, and most of them don't, really. You know? People who have had those close encounters of one sort or another.

DENNIS: I believe that.

JERRY: It changes their lives because, what would you do? I mean, if you were driving along and here's this big silver object in the middle of the freeway, you know, in the middle of the night. There's nobody around but you, and they shine a weird light on you, and you lose maybe two or three hours of your life to some peculiar thing, and maybe under hypnosis it comes out that you've been taken aboard this craft—you know what I mean? This is truly weird shit.

DENNIS: Because you'd spend the rest of your life sitting around saying, "Why me?"

JERRY: Right.

45

DENNIS: "What does this mean?"

JERRY: Right. Exactly right. And you may never figure it out, and in fact most people don't, and it tends to warp you. And just somebody who is willing to say, there are such experiences and people actually do have them, and so at least, you know, let's show that. Even though the rest of it is fiction, you know, the coming together with them and all the rest of that stuff, is something else entirely. But the accurate depiction of them—you know what I mean? And that stuff in the beginning with the traffic controllers and all that. I just appreciated that, and the thing that they were—that he used music as a language.

DENNIS: Right. That was the hippest thing because—

JERRY: As a musician I appreciated that.

DENNIS: Well, it's the universal [language], I mean, how would we—?

JERRY: It may be. I mean, we have no way of knowing. And besides—

DENNIS: Assuming ETs could hear.

JERRY: Yeah, the whole thing about flying saucers, of course, is it's much more likely that they're a local part of the environment and not from out there. So what they are and who's responsible, or if any consciousness at all is involved or rather, what they are, you know?

DENNIS: Yeah.

JERRY: That is not known. So the whole thing about unidentified flying objects is they're unidentified. But at least, I love the fact that they went on the trip of making it look the way the reports look, having the people react the way the reports say they react, and that [kind of] thing. The thing of normal people in an abnormal situation, something I've always loved. So I waited for that movie to come out. I really did. And you know, there is an interesting series of teeny-weeny coincidences that go along with that. I'll tell you about it. Do you know who Jacques Vallee is? [Vallee is a scientist who worked on the mapping of Mars for NASA and was part of developing ARPANET, a precursor to the Internet; he also studies UFOs and at least allowed for the possibility of an extraterrestrial explanation.] Jacques Vallee is one of the few real scientists who's involved in the flying saucer stuff. The Lacombe character [in *Close Encounters*]—

DENNIS: Right.
JERRY: You know, the French character?

DENNIS: Right.
JERRY: He's sort of patterned after Jacques Vallee, who is actually a computer guy, a computer scientist, but he's an astrophysicist. He's a young guy, not very old, and he and Allen Hynek are the two scientists who are most seriously involved, scientifically, with the flying saucer phenomenon. Okay. I just read this article by Jacques Vallee in a magazine, where he was talking about coincidence, and in this article he says he's been studying a character, a biblical character called Melchizedek in the Bible.

DENNIS: Mm-hmm.
JERRY: And he had been in Europe and he had just flown to L.A. International Airport, got picked up by a cabdriver, a girl. The cabdriver's name was Melchizedek. He found out from looking at her receipt the next day. He looked in the phonebook and there was only two Melchizedeks in Los Angeles.

DENNIS: Even in L.A.
JERRY: Two Melchizedeks. So he's talking about, now, coincidence. He doesn't think there is such a thing as coincidence. He thinks there is a net of probability of some sort. Now, here's the thing: when *Close Encounters* came out, we were booked at the hotel on the street corner opposite the theater where it opened in New York, where it opened ten days before general release. It was at the Ziegfeld Theatre, and I was there with my band and we were playing at the Academy of Music [later the Palladium]. And while I was at the Academy of Music, the— Oh, also, at the beginning of this Vallee article, he's talking a little about extraterrestrials. He talks about *Saturday Night Live*. He says—he says –

DENNIS: The Coneheads.

JERRY: Right. When the Coneheads are asked where they come from, they say from France. Which is where Vallee comes from.

DENNIS: Oh, right. Okay.

JERRY: Okay. So I'm down there at the Academy of Music and these guys come up the stairs and say, "Hey, would you okay this Conehead poster because Connie Conehead wears a Grateful Dead T-shirt?" So they needed my permission to be able to put it out, so that's where I started to get to know [Al] Franken and [Tom] Davis, one of the *Saturday Night Live* guys. Here I am dealing with *Saturday Night Live*, which I just read about in this article about coincidence, which happens to be where *Close Encounters* opens across the street during the same stretch of time. So it's this little network of bizarre coincidences having to do with flying saucers, *Saturday Night Live*, the Coneheads, Jacques Vallee, France, you know. All of these other things are all drawn together, weirdly, kind of in this weird network of coincidences, like the coincidences that he writes about in his article about Melchizedek. You know? That stuff. . . .

So it was like one of those things like being in Egypt when the moon eclipsed. [The Grateful Dead performed in Egypt in 1978 and on their last night, there was an eclipse of the moon. See Chapter Eight for more detail.] For me, it's that kind of thing, because my mind was going over this shit. You know what I mean? That was the stuff that was on my mind, and all these things came together, and I never used to watch *Saturday Night Live*. So I didn't know from the Coneheads. You know? The only way I knew about the Coneheads was by reading about them in this article by Vallee. And really, the introduction in the article, it talks about Vallee. It talks about him and it talks about the coincidence business and it talks about the Coneheads there. So it's—I mean, it's just, you know, one of those improbable trails of coincidence.

DENNIS: Right. Good synchronicity.

JERRY: Right. That's it. Synchronicity.

DENNIS: Yeah, sometimes it gets a little more obvious.

JERRY: There may have been more to it, but I don't remember.

DENNIS: Yeah.

JERRY: There was a lot happening at that particular moment, and, you know, I was in the zone myself, but it was a great moment, just one of those great moments.

DENNIS: That's lovely.

JERRY: It was really good. Me and Candelario went to see that movie about six times during the week. It was right down the street. You know? We could go out. There were no lines or anything. It was the easiest thing in the world to just go over there. And the movie was so great looking on the big screen, brand new print.

Frankenstein at the Lab.
Mixed media on paper.

DENNIS: Yeah, it was the most elegant—

JERRY: It was also—oh, that's right. It was also at the Ziegfeld Theatre where our movie premiered, too.

DENNIS: Right.

JERRY: That's where we were—just opposite the Ziegfeld Theatre. It was just, you know, one of those things, like a perfect moment.

2

Getting Launched on the "Rosy Road to Hell"

Submarines. Pencil on paper.

Any number of influences pushed Garcia away from a conventional mind-set to that of an iconoclastic seeker who grew to be the artist we'd all come to know. Media was a major factor—records, film, television—but there were also two teachers in particular who encouraged his talents and expanded his perspective. The first was Miss Simon, his third-grade teacher, who recognized his artistic eye and fostered his talent. Years later he'd salute her for giving him the encouragement to locate his identity as an artist, as someone not average, as someone who was different, and happy about that.

At the same time Miss Simon was working her magic, he found another visual inspiration in the EC Comics his brother, Tiff, first showed him. "EC" stood for Entertaining Comics, and they featured titles like *Tales from the Crypt* and *The Vault of Horror*, a genre both written and cinematic that he'd love for the rest of his life.

The other teacher who inspired young Jerry was quite different from Miss Simon. For a brief period in Jerry's early teens, his family had lived in suburban Menlo Park, which soon proved vapid and boring to Jerry, a natural city kid. Dwight Johnson was Jerry's seventh-grade teacher. And Mr. Johnson had style. He drove an MG TC or a Vincent Black Shadow motorcycle—as Jerry put it, "pretty racy stuff" for Menlo Park. Johnson engaged Jerry's mind with big questions—the meaning of life, the relationship of the individual to society—through the literature of George Orwell and D. H. Lawrence, and by the end of seventh grade, Jerry's mind and ambitions had expanded well beyond the world of Menlo Park.

TOP: Cat and Mouse Games.
Pen and ink on paper.

BOTTOM: Cartoon Cop.
Pen and ink on paper.

Naturally, if you're going to talk with Jerry Garcia, you're going to talk about music. Rhythm and blues—R&B—and eventually rock 'n' roll were the primary music of his life in the early '50s. The first song he remembered from that time was "Gee," by the Crows, a street-corner doo-wop tune that he cherished. In June 1957, his family had moved back to San Francisco, and he lived with his mother and stepfather above the bar she owned on the corner (various corners, actually) of First and Harrison, near downtown and close to the waterfront. There he listened to music on the jukebox, and on the transistor radio that was semipermanently plugged into his ear.

The conversation below starts with Jerry talking about the history of EC Comics, and the sources of their style and plots.

 | Start of Interview

JERRY: [It's] really—innovative. Look at this kind of stuff just in terms of the, you know, exaggerations and stuff. These kind of things, these cinematic kind of things.

DENNIS: Uh huh.

JERRY: And this kind of open framing down here. This stuff was really wild in the fifties.

DENNIS: And it was very odd for cartooning.

JERRY: Right. But then I loved these guys. This guy had a style that was based on, like, silent movies, like, he has this really wonderful fine line—fine brush—all this fine-line brush, dynamic brushstroke style that's full of expressionistic shit, like these kind of high-angle shots with a lot of shadow. And tremendous attention and stuff in these drawings. They're so good.

DENNIS: Mm-hmm.

JERRY: I mean, this stuff is so much better than comic artwork is nowadays.

DENNIS: Oh, yeah. Even Saturday morning cartoons are like . . . After growing up on Warner Brothers and Bullwinkle, to look at the kind of crap they put out now.

JERRY: Yeah, it doesn't even compare. I mean—

52

Various Scenes of Horror.
Mixed media on paper.

DENNIS: It's embarrassing.

JERRY: Yeah, it really is. Yeah, right, it is embarrassing. But these are the guys that made me conscious of style, I think, really, without knowing it. And also, these things are pretty literate, too. You know? They use a lot of big words, and there's a lot of text to each of the stories. See all those paragraphs and text for each panel?

DENNIS: They all lift a lot from, like, Poe and Lovecraft.

JERRY: Oh yeah, definitely. Very definitely

DENNIS: Between the two you got pretty literate—

JERRY: Right. And these stories are straight Old Testament stuff, you know what I mean? It's an eye for an eye in these babies. They're very moralistic. They're straight moral plays.Because these things formed some part of my taste and character, that's one of the reasons why I collected them—I mean, why I re-collected them. You know?

54

DENNIS: Uh huh.

JERRY: To see what was warping my mind as a kid. You know?

⟩⟩⟩ ⟨⟨⟨

JERRY: It's interesting to run into the furniture of your childhood. You know what I mean? The psychic furniture of your childhood. I mean, for me, these comic books meant a lot because I was sick. I was a sickly kid.

> **"It's interesting to run into the furniture of your childhood. You know what I mean? The psychic furniture of your childhood."**

DENNIS: Right.

JERRY: And I spent more days sick in bed with my EC comic books than I care to tell about, you know what I mean? Really a lot of them. Probably fifty percent of the days of an average school year.

DENNIS: That much?

JERRY: Yeah. I was really a sickly kid. Asthma dominated my life. It really did. I couldn't run, you know? I could barely walk up a flight of stairs without really getting exhausted. I was a sick kid.

DENNIS: Endlessly frustrating—

JERRY: That's who I was, so it really restricted my ability to play with other kids, and I didn't socialize that well, you know? Not until I was a little older. And then I never had much trouble, but I was a loner when I was a little kid, and reading was my life. You know what I mean? That was where my mind went. I was lucky. I might never have read if it wasn't for being sick.

>>> <<<

DENNIS: Did you ever read the newspaper?

JERRY: Yeah, sure. I used to read Herb Caen. My grandmother was a big Herb Caen fan. Yeah, she loved Herb Caen. But I was not what you would describe as socially conscious. I had a kind of, what I guess must have been a bohemian teacher when I was in the third grade who was probably the first person who kicked me down the rosy road to hell, you know? She was a great teacher named Miss Simon. She was young and pretty and she always wore flowery peasant dresses. She must have been a bohemian at the time.

TOP: Foxtrot TH4 Romeo Crybaby Circus.
Colored pencils on paper.

BOTTOM: Reluctant Dragon.
Colored pencils on paper.

DENNIS: Secret boho, right.

JERRY: And she was the one who encouraged me to do the creative stuff. She liked my drawings, and she really encouraged me along those lines, and she had me involved in every kind of art project there was around. You know? And she definitely steered me in that direction. She was the first person to really give me that, and that gave me my first identity as an artist. She was the first person to think of me as an artist and to get me functioning as an artist, and so I became an artist, you know, in my own mind. And that was probably one of the most important turn-ons—that was probably what left me open enough for everything else, and also started me on the road to really thinking of myself as being different from other people. Miss Simon. I'll always remember Miss Simon.

⋙ ⋘

The next segment of conversation comes from the 1973 session with Al Aronowitz and Jerry's unidentified woman friend.

JERRY: And so [Miss Simon] put me to work drawing stuff. I used a lot of energy, and I started to understand something about doing what you enjoy doing and what you can do well, you know, and working at it. That was, like, my first flash of that.

And then there was nothing, a long period of nothing. And then when I moved out of San Francisco down to the peninsula, which is like the suburbs anywhere. You know, it's homogenous; there's no real character to what's going on. And this was down near Palo Alto, Menlo Park.

And um, I had a teacher in the seventh grade named Dwight Johnson, and this guy, I think—this guy is an interesting guy all by himself in a small way. Do you know who Ed McClanahan is? He's a writer, a friend of [Ken] Kesey's. He's a good friend of Kesey's—

DENNIS: He did the article on you guys in *Playboy*.

JERRY: Yeah, and he teaches or something down at Stanford. But at the time that I was in the seventh grade, this guy, Ed McClanahan, was starting at Stanford.

And this guy who was my teacher, Dwight Johnson, was a famous freak at Stanford. He was, like, really an unconventional person. He had, like, an MG TC, you know, and a Vincent Black Shadow. You know what I mean? He was, like, pretty racy for that scene at that time. And he used to—in the seventh grade down in the suburban school, he was always bringing up and we were always getting into, like, controversial crazy shit, you know, in class, which finally created a scandal, and subsequently he was fired for discussing something, you know, in class. And he's the one that turned me on to, like, reading. I mean, like really, you know, heavy stuff, like first, those opening flashes, when you start to suspect that the world is not the way that you've been taught, and it's like, by reading stuff like George Orwell and that kind of stuff. You know, those first primary little steps, and then that kind of stuff, and then into heavier and heavier stuff.

Dog Beating Pan.
Pen and ink on paper.

57

And that, like, really spun me out completely from school, you know what I mean? At that point, me and school were on two completely different . . . I was on a, like, total iconoclast, you know, really caught up in that flash of, you know, intellectual awakening. You know, like the first year of college or something like that. Anyway . . .

But that was the point at which I departed from the regular world. And then from there was like the thing, my interest in art had been going on steadily and ended up with me moving back to the city, my mother moving back to the city and everything, and me going to art school, like, a couple of days a week in addition to going to regular school in San Francisco. And school in San Francisco at that time [Denman Junior High School, Balboa High School] was the jungle, right?

AL: Right.

JERRY: It was the *Blackboard Jungle* [a 1955 film about gritty inner-city youth that heralded the arrival of rock 'n' roll by playing Bill Haley's "Rock Around the

Clock" over the opening credits and elsewhere]. And it was that whole movie going on. And so, like, in school, regular high school, you know, I was just like every other hoodlum—except for when I would go to my art classes.

〉〉〉 〈〈〈

JERRY: And all this time I was living on First Street, like downtown San Francisco, like by skid row, and taking a bus all the way across town to go to this one high school because my grandmother lived near there and I could go into the district—because my mother didn't like the high schools in the neighborhood. So I was living by the waterfront in my mother's place going to art school, you know, and getting off in that world and then drudging through high school.

AL: Well, did it have to be like a secret world for the hoodlums?

JERRY: Well, for example, if my hoodlum friends came over to my house and saw my paintings, they'd rip them up and shit. So I had to keep it all kind of undercover.

58

Jerry, c. 1952.

AL: Like, with that gang, if you painted or wrote poems, you were a sissy.
JERRY: Right. It wasn't really cool to do that.

AL: So you had to really keep it like a whole secret life then.
JERRY: Yeah. Well, yeah, except that I wasn't able to do that, so everything else
       started slipping.

AL: Right.
JERRY: You know, everything started slipping.

〉〉〉 〈〈〈

DENNIS: Where did you plug into the R&B trip? Do you remember?
JERRY: It was just in the air, really. I don't remember really when it started.

DENNIS: Was it radio?
JERRY: I remember the first song I liked was "Gee" by the Crows [singing]. And it had
       a real, it had a real street kind of voice. That guy's voice was . . . it had a real
       street voice. And I remember the sound of it was—yeah. Yeah.

59

DENNIS: I like that.
JERRY: It was one of those things that, yeah, that's it. That's the stuff, you know, as
       a doo-wop group, the Crows sounded great. And it still sounds badass, too. I
       might have a copy of it somewhere. No, I don't. I know I don't. But it's around,
       I'm sure, and that's the—that's it. That was the first tune that I remember.
       And then came stuff which, to me, is kind of like noise in the system, but it
       all of a sudden, you know, jumped out, all that Bill Haley stuff. And I never
       liked it that much, but what I did like was the way "Rock Around the Clock"
       sounded when it was at the beginning of *Blackboard Jungle*.

DENNIS: I was going to say, did you see that movie?
JERRY: Sure.

Jerry in high school, c. 1960.

60

DENNIS: That was one of the—

JERRY: Because it was the only one where the kids in it looked like the kids in school did, you know? I mean, they looked real, finally, and, you know . . .

DENNIS: Did you see *Rebel Without a Cause* at that time?

JERRY: That was later. [Interestingly, both movies came out in 1955.] That was quite a lot later. It was a lot later as far as its effect, you know? I was a James Dean fan. I was a big James Dean fan. I mean—

DENNIS: From everything you said, you sort of logically—

JERRY: Yeah, I was a big James Dean fan. But that—for me, that was much later. For me, that—

DENNIS: But "Rock Around the Clock" was—

JERRY: The grit of that, the way it worked in that picture, I liked. But I didn't really like the tune that much. I've never liked Bill Haley that much. For me, I liked the black stuff better, you know. And at that time, like the "Shake, Rattle and Roll"—there was a "Shake, Rattle and Roll" that Bill Haley and the Comets did, and there was a "Shake, Rattle and Roll" that Joe Turner did. There was an R&B version out about that same time that I liked much, much better.

DENNIS: Yeah.

JERRY: And it was at that time that I started to be conscious, "Oh, I see, there's the black version of stuff that's good and then there's the lame white version of stuff sometimes," you know.

DENNIS: Right.

JERRY: And then they came out with all these things that were like "Work with Me, Annie," Hank Ballard and the Midnighters and that stuff, the early R&B stuff. And there were also these nice R&B groups that came out from—that were affected, I guess—they were from Korea, guys that had been, soldiers that had been in Korea. So there were tunes—they were sort of novelty tunes that had, like, a few Korean licks in them, Korean words and stuff like that.

DENNIS: Oh.

JERRY: And that's the earliest stuff I can remember being affected by, that early R&B, and I liked that. I guess my brother must have introduced it around, you know. I guess that's how I must have started hearing it.

DENNIS: Did you buy records?

JERRY: I didn't buy records until later. I didn't have money.

DENNIS: Right.

JERRY: But as soon as I started to realize there were radios that you can listen to, and radio stations . . . It was around then that there started being radio stations that played nothing but music. Television started taking over the narrative form. Before that, radio was plays.

DENNIS: Mix.

JERRY: Yeah, there was the mix. So about [that] time, I started being conscious of those stations that played music. So for me, that meant KWBR and KDIA— they were the two R&B stations in the area. And I preferred the one in Oakland, KWBR. And I just . . . my ear fell into it, you know?

DENNIS: Ate it up.

JERRY: Oh, man. Yeah, I sure did. I remember when Ray Charles first came out. And in those days, there were even guys like John Lee Hooker and Jimmy Reed, I mean, really raw. And even Lightnin' Hopkins had songs that they played a lot on the radio. They were, like, radio hits, R&B hits. In those days, there was really rhythm and blues on the radio. There was really blues, and B. B. King you heard real regular, and then it was real raw and there was a lot more to it then. It was much more interesting.

DENNIS: Really.

JERRY: And I mean, that's all I listened to when I—into that teenage space. For me, that was heaven, you know?

DENNIS: So then I would presume that, what, "Maybellene"—

JERRY: Then I liked rock 'n' roll when that started, which was actually later, you know?

DENNIS: Oh, yeah.

JERRY: And I liked it when it came in. You know, when these white guys were playing rock 'n' roll, hey, playing R&B, yeah, that's cool. "Maybellene," I remember when that first came out. That was really a different sound, you know, it was all of a sudden very different. When I first heard it, I thought it was kind of like a cowboy song, except it was nastier, you know?

DENNIS: Old Chuck.

JERRY: Yeah, yeah.

DENNIS: I must say that one of the things that makes the Grateful Dead interesting and easy to write about is, unlike virtually every other group of artists, you guys have sufficient, incredible, each individual, variety of musical [interests], and you were into the whole R&B thing for, like, five good years before Chuck Berry recorded a lick.

JERRY: That's right. Really, I really listened to it.

DENNIS: And when you were playing with Etta James, [On December 31, 1982, Etta opened for the Grateful Dead, and they closed the show by backing her.] I was just flashing on that as, you know, I had a visual sense of moving it to a little bar on Mission Street, and it would have been—

JERRY: Hey, I could have been there and been perfectly happy.

DENNIS: Right.

JERRY: I could have been there. Lived my whole life there and been perfectly happy, yeah, sure.

>>> <<<

Race Record Dream.
Mixed media on paper.

DENNIS: Your father's bar was called Joe's Place, right?

JERRY: I don't know.

DENNIS: Okay. Do you remember the jukebox at all?

JERRY: I don't remember the jukebox when my father had it.

DENNIS: No. Back when you were . . . like in the late fifties.

JERRY: Sure.

DENNIS: What kind of stuff was in the jukebox? What was it called then? Do you remember that?

JERRY: It didn't have a name.

DENNIS: No? Okay.

JERRY: Okay. No, it didn't have a name at all. When my mother owned it and it moved from the first . . . That's where the SUP [Sailors' Union of the Pacific, 450 Harrison St., corner of First Street] is now, and that was when my father had it. My mother sold it, sold the property, and the SUP was built there, and she got the next corner where the 76 [Union Oil Co.] building is now. [Since the time of this interview, the 76 Union building has been replaced by One Rincon Center, an apartment building.] And that was during like, I guess, '50, to maybe '54, somewhere around there and we moved to the peninsula.

DENNIS: Right.

JERRY: She sold it around there and we moved to the next corner.

DENNIS: Right.

JERRY: And she got the other corner—

DENNIS: The third corner. The Naugahyde one, the fancy one. You and Tiff worked there.

JERRY: That's right and that's—

DENNIS: With the dogs on the roof.

JERRY: Yeah, right, it was pretty plain, really. It was just a workingman's bar, it was just open during the day. It closed when the union hall closed, pretty much, and a few of the executives, the stronger-willed executives from [the] 76 would come down and hang out with the sailors who drank there. And it was fun. It was a nice bar.

DENNIS: As I said, the jukebox—

JERRY: The jukebox was good. One of the ones that I remember at the second bar was one that you tell what you want to hear. There was an operator of some kind. I don't know how they did it. They must have had a central place with lots of records and actual disk jockeys of some sort. I couldn't figure out. I've never been able to figure out .

DENNIS: It was like the Muzak setup.

JERRY: Feasible, yeah. Yes. I mean, there was a trip of trying to stump the lady. There was a lady who would come on and ask you what you wanted to hear, and you would say whatever it was. And I remember trying to stump it. This is the early fifties.

DENNIS: Right.

JERRY: That didn't last very long. That was the weirdest jukebox I remember.

DENNIS: Really.

JERRY: It didn't have records in it. It was a big chrome thing and it had a little speaker on it like this and it had a little microphone on it down there somewhere and you put in a quarter or whatever it was. It might have been fifty cents,

Joe at the family bar, c. mid-1940s.

I don't remember. It was expensive for a jukebox at the time. I mean, this was back with the nickel jukebox days.

DENNIS: Right.

JERRY: But then the jukebox over at the last bar—there was also a piano there, my mom's upright piano, that I used to play after hours and fuck around with, and I used to listen to Jerry Lee Lewis on the jukebox, and Buddy Holly.

Joe's band. Date unknown.

But sometimes I'd bring my electric guitar down there. And when I was sweeping up after the place was closed . . . then it was my scene, you know? And that was fun. Those were songs that . . . That was already the time of the early transistor radios.

DENNIS: Mm-hmm.

JERRY: And I was one of those guys who had a little transistor radio plugged into my ear, you know, one of those things . . . I was seriously strung out on music during the early rock 'n' roll.

DENNIS: So the jukebox, they had rock 'n' roll?

JERRY: Oh, yeah, sure. It had some lame stuff, but it had mostly rock 'n' roll, you know? I mean, that was the time when the jukebox business and rock 'n' roll were pretty much tight. It was still, I guess, in the days when rock 'n' roll was basically crooked, you know? All along, too, as long as there were jukeboxes, I got records from them. The jukebox guys, when they changed the records, sometimes I would get the old records. A lot of the records were totally terrible, but that was the way I got Carl Perkins's version of "Blue Suede Shoes" when we lived down on the peninsula. I got [it] in a little pile of funky 45s.

DENNIS: Uh huh.

JERRY: And a couple of other kind of nice things. You know?

DENNIS: I found a copy of your first R&B record, "Gee."

JERRY: Oh, yeah? The Crows! [Jerry and M. G. sing the opening of "Gee"] Yeah, sure. That was an important song. That was the first kind of, like where the voices had that kind of not-trained-singer voices, but tough-guy-on-the-street voice.

DENNIS: Yeah. Definitely street corner.

JERRY: Yeah. That was definitely a change from the stuff you heard on the radio. And it was important. And then white port lemon juice, "W.P.L.J." [The Four Deuces.] That was one of my anthem songs when I was in junior high school and high school and around there. That was one of those songs everybody knew. And that everybody sang. Everybody sang that street-corner favorite.

DENNIS: You mentioned there was a radio station from Oakland—

JERRY: Yeah.

DENNIS: —that you listened to the most, the blues and the R&B stuff.

JERRY: KWBR.

DENNIS: It is KWBR?

JERRY: I think so. It used to be. I always thought that WB must be Warner Brothers, but it probably wasn't. And it had Bouncin' Bill Doubleday on it. It didn't have George Oxford, Jumpin' George. He was on KDIA in San Francisco. There were two R&B stations, but I listened mostly to KWBR.

DENNIS: Okay.

JERRY: And that was in the days when they used to play, like, John Lee Hooker and Jimmy Reed, I mean funky stuff. You know? Muddy Waters and Jimmy McCracklin and all this kind of blues and B. B. King. It was back when rhythm and blues meant blues, rhythm and blues.

DENNIS: Right, with the accent on blues.

JERRY: And also the first Ray Charles records. The first couple of those. I remember "Lonely Avenue" was one of the first ones. I remember really liking "I Got a Woman." I don't know which one of them was his first one. But I remember when his sound appeared, it was like something new, something really fresh. I mean, everything was of course totally a mystery. I was completely naive about records and all that; I was just a kid, you know? But I remember noting the different feelings that different records had, the different styles, the bands, the way they . . . you know? The way the records themselves sounded, the textures of them. And it was one of those things that I always . . . if I had known how to form the questions, it was one of those things I wanted to know about, because it was real obvious to me I couldn't even make my friends understand it. You know? It was one of those things [like], "Sit down and listen to this record and listen to how that thing sounds there." I didn't know what I was listening to, but what I was listening to was things like the tone of the echo chamber.

Jerry in front of the family bar, c. 1950.

DENNIS: Uh huh.

JERRY: You know, the kind of repeat slap echo that was big on early rock 'n' roll records, things like that. I know what they are now, but I didn't know what they were then. But I remember listening to them and wondering, and those things were an important part of why I liked certain records and why I liked the sounds of things.

Jerry on Community

Whatever its name or lack thereof, the bar at the corner of First and Harrison deeply influenced Jerry by becoming the first of the communities he would belong to. It was a workingman's bar in what was then a blue-collar workingman's town, directly across the street from the headquarters of the Sailors' Union of the Pacific. A central part of the SUP's heritage profoundly honored the memory of the two strikers killed twenty years before just a few blocks down the hill on "Bloody Thursday," during the city's great strike of 1934. Plenty of the men at the bar had been part of that strike, and they treated Jerry as family. They included him in conversations and listened to what he had to say. These conversations left him with a deep respect for unions (more on that in Chapter Seven), skeptical toward government and police, and with a genuinely democratic attitude toward everybody.

Jerry extended this attitude to the Grateful Dead's road crew. The relationship between bands and their crew members is often fairly corporate; the tour manager hires and fires the staff, and there can be a lot of turnover. That was not the way it was with the Dead, and that's at least partly attributable to Jerry. The Dead's crew—most notably Lawrence "Ram Rod" Shurtliff, Steve Parish, Bill "Kidd" Candelario, and Billy Grillo—were part of the band. Ram Rod was an exceptional man, and it was no accident that he eventually became the president of the Grateful Dead Corporation—he was simply that trusted. Crew opinions affected touring decisions—if they hated a venue, it was unlikely to be used again.

The Grateful Dead family consisted of more than just the crew, of course. The (mostly) women of the office were also respected, and the idea of community extended all the way to the audience. And it wasn't just Jerry. As the Grateful Dead passed through the trial-by-fire called the Acid Tests, they experienced something unique. Over two months between December 1965 and January 1966 (there were some Acid Tests after that in Los Angeles, but they were largely anticlimactic), Ken Kesey and the Merry Pranksters and the Dead brought together groups of people to take LSD together. For those events, the

69

Dead were *not* the show. They were free to play or not. The show was everyone in the room; the Dead, along with the Prankster "Band," merely provided the soundtrack. But even when they played to sixty thousand people in a giant stadium, the band would remember that the audience was not a passive bunch of adoring fans, but partners in a quest. Now *that's* a community.

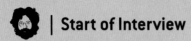 ## | Start of Interview

JERRY: He's real spare on coming out and doing stuff like that, but it does make you feel good when Ram Rod compliments you.

DENNIS: Yeah.

JERRY: Or gives you that handshake or claps you on the back. It's like, he's a real pardoner, you know? He's one of those guys . . . You know what Ram Rod's like. Ram Rod represents a kind of high-water integrity marker, you know?

DENNIS: Yup.

JERRY: He's—

DENNIS: He's the conscience.

JERRY: He sure is, and he takes it very seriously.

DENNIS: Amen. He gets those little reading glasses . . .

JERRY: You know, I bust him. He's straighter than I'd be, you know, and I can be awful straight in that kind of position. And even I will tell him, "Hey, let up a little bit," you know? He's a great guy.

DENNIS: Yeah. It's amazing. The thing that's intriguing is that I know that there is no other band in the world that has—in him in particular, most obviously, in him, Parish in some ways, but in particular him and Healy—the level of influence and the recognition from the musicians that they're part of the trip. Not to mention all the rest of us employees—you know, band meetings that include everybody.

JERRY: Well, you've got to figure just because you're a musician doesn't mean you're smarter than anybody else. It doesn't mean you're better or smarter or anything than anybody else. Do you know what I mean? Being a musician is just a matter of choice. It certainly doesn't entitle you to anything. Wisdom is where you find it, you know . . . every point of view at its very worst will see something that you don't see. I mean, people are stupid if they don't use everything that's there, you know what I mean? When you've got people, you know, whole human beings, and they care enough about what you're doing to put some part of their life and their energy into it, shit, the least you can do is to let them help shape it and direct it as much as they care to.

DENNIS: That's, of course, a totally reasonable and righteous attitude. And you also know that quite often, you know, Mick Jagger don't listen to nobody, as an example, from what I understand.

JERRY: Well, I guess, if he feels he can handle the responsibility all by himself, more power to him, you know. But I personally wouldn't want the responsibility, you know? I wouldn't care to have that many people waiting around to see what I wanted them to do. You know what I mean? I would feel awful if I made wrong decisions. And I wouldn't care to do that. I've already been through that in my head.

DENNIS: Well, it's the difference between a hierarch[y] and the closest thing to anarchy. Working, functioning anarchy.

JERRY: Right.

DENNIS: Not anarchy, but anarchism . . .

JERRY: Well, working, functioning anarchism means that whoever's got it is the guy that leads right at that moment, whoever sees it clearest at that moment. And I have had enough experience by now to know that sometimes it's Candelario, you know. Sometimes,

> "Well, you've got to figure just because you're a musician doesn't mean you're smarter than anybody else."

71

it's places you'd never expect it to be. But you don't know unless you leave the door open.

DENNIS: Well, that's why having the general band meetings . . . that's part of what I mean by morale. Because everybody is just right there and everybody goes to those meetings feeling . . . nobody feels like they're going to get slapped down.

JERRY: Right.

DENNIS: And I know that some of the women; Eileen [Law, a staff member who particularly took care of Dead Heads] had recalled being requested to come to a band meeting once and asking a question. And Sparky [Raizene, a crew member]—this is years ago, ten years ago—really dumped on her. And she mentioned that to me and remarked recently, you know, that there's just none of that sense anymore. Everybody's in a space to be semi-reasonable and "let's get things done" and you know, think about it.

JERRY: Absolutely. We're all in this together, you know. It's our toy.

DENNIS: And there's only a limited amount of energy, and you might as well use it as efficiently as possible.

JERRY: Lets everybody have all their dreams fulfilled. You know what I mean? It's like if we have a vehicle to dreams, let's knock 'em down, you know. Let's set 'em up and knock 'em down. You know what I mean? This life is what we can do with it, I guess. I mean, it seems to be encouraging us to do that. So as long as it's going that way, let's do it that way. Let's be good to ourselves. Let's be good to each other. I wouldn't know what else to do in life. It would be a terrible bummer to not be able to go through life with your friends anyway. That's what the very start was about, you know.

DENNIS: Yeah. It's just that one thing, the whole notion of playing with friends.

JERRY: Yeah, really.

DENNIS: Of music as a conversation, musical conversation amongst five or six people, you know. To me, that's, on a certain level, the essence of the Grateful Dead. And the point is, it is music created by musicians, not performers. You know, Mick Jagger is a great performer and the Rolling Stones, you know, it's a performance. And that means it's structured and it's the same.

JERRY: Hey, there is nothing wrong with performances. Performance is a great trip. There is an art of performance.

DENNIS: But performance is for entertainment, and that's not what the Grateful Dead are about.

JERRY: It's just another type of thing. Right.

DENNIS: The Grateful Dead are entertaining.

JERRY: It just has another sense to it. It can be entertaining, I guess. You know, certainly entertaining to me at times.

DENNIS: Oh, yeah.

JERRY: But it's a lot of other things, too. Some full-range thing, you know . . . I like for it to be whatever anybody wants for it to be.

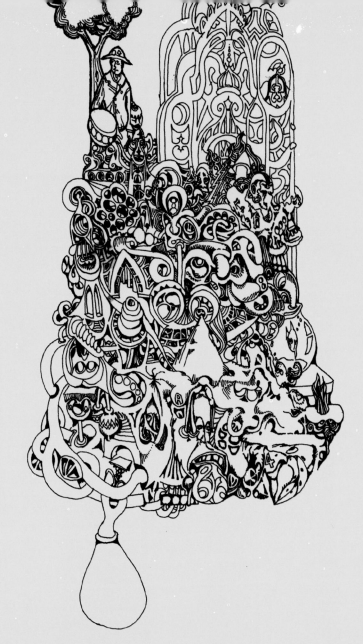

3

The Keys to Heaven, and then the Army

Architectural Doodle/Early Work.
Pen and ink on paper.

North Beach is a special neighborhood within San Francisco. From the end of World War II on, this largely Italian enclave also became the low-rent yet charming home of disaffected painters and poets. As the 1950s came to be symbolized nationally by the television program *Father Knows Best*, North Beach became home to raffish bars like The Place, which catered to poets with a weekly "Blabbermouth Night" where anyone could get up and spout their art. At the heart of North Beach's appeal was the California School of Fine Arts (now the San Francisco Art Institute), which flanked the neighborhood from the side of Russian Hill. Jerry Garcia became himself there—it was the only school he ever attended that he was proud to claim.

Having returned to the city in the summer of 1957, he began taking weekend and evening classes at the Institute, and the proximity to important artists like Elmer Bischoff, Mark Rothko, and Clyfford Still inspired him. His primary teacher was a man named Wally Hedrick, who created "funk art" assemblages, played guitar and traditional jazz banjo, and had his young students listen to music as they painted. Hedrick had been part of a late '40s/early '50s poetry scene called the San Francisco Renaissance led by Robert Duncan, which had opened an art gallery on Fillmore Street first called the King Ubu Gallery, and then the Six Gallery.

It was Wally who came up with the idea of a poetry reading at the Six Gallery, and eventually it fell to a New York immigrant by the name of Allen Ginsberg to organize it. On October 7, 1955, six poets read; the highlight of the evening was Ginsberg's first public reading of "Howl," the most important American poem of the twentieth century. Just as Jerry got to art school two years later, Ginsberg's friend Jack Kerouac published his book *On the Road*, and it became a national best-seller, helping introduce the phrase "Beat Generation" to America. The Beats soon became identifiable as a gaggle of disaffected artists who wanted a more soulful and spiritual America rather than the one in which they were living—a world diving headfirst into the good life of conformist suburban prosperity in an effort to make up for the deprivations of the Depression, World War II, and Cold War McCarthyism. The Beats were ripe for satire, as berets, goatees, hip slang, and the TV character Maynard G. Krebs made clear. Wally Hedrick made money by sitting in the front window of the touristy Beat bar Vesuvio Café—he had a beard, which meant the tourists could identify the place as Beat just by seeing him.

But for Jerry, it was the beginning of a permanent commitment to a life centered on art (both graphic and musical) and the spirit. He was, he thought, the youngest Beat. It was Wally who influenced him to pick up the guitar, which he got—

75

eventually—for his fifteenth birthday in August 1957. Once that Danelectro electric guitar was in Jerry's hands, his future was assured, even if the learning was slow.

One of the other new things in his life was pot, which he discovered that same summer of 1957 (quite a summer!). This deviation from the norm disturbed his mother, and in 1959 she tried to save her wayward son by moving them to the tiny rural town of Cazadero, two hours and ninety long miles north of San Francisco. The move did put Jerry in his first band, but it was no surprise when he quit school and did the normal thing for a young man in late '50s America with no particular prospects: he joined the army. See the world! It was a memorable, if not exactly triumphant, "career."

**This first portion of this interview comes from the 1973 session with
Al Aronowitz and the unidentified woman friend.**

 | Start of Interview

AL: When did you tell me was your first awareness that something was going on up in North Beach?

JERRY: Well, when I was really young. When I was a little kid . . .

AL: You were sick, and I think you were fourteen. You started reading.

JERRY: That was when I . . . well, I was reading. Yeah, when I was fourteen was when I got turned on, when I got turned on to a whole other world. That's when I first flashed on it. But in San Francisco, North Beach is always—even when I was a little kid—always represented like a kind of far-out place. But it wasn't until—well, actually, my first exposure to any of that was when I was taking art classes. I was going to what's now the San Francisco Art Institute. It used to be the California School of Fine Arts, and I went there like a couple of nights a week. Like a night school thing. And it was, like, where the painters were, and it was in North Beach. So, you know, it was immediately, like, the art set in San Francisco. And that was my exposure to it. And out of that, you know, is when I first heard about the word "Beat." And it was before the beatnik thing, before Herb Caen was talking about . . .

AL: How did you hear the word "Beat"?

JERRY: A teacher, a guy named Wally Hedrick.

AL: Yeah.

JERRY: Who's a good painter in San Francisco and also plays guitar.

AL: Yeah.

JERRY: Just, you know, he mentioned that that was like . . .

AL: Yeah, I met Wally.

JERRY: —it came up in some kind of a rap.

AL: Yeah.

JERRY: Some kind of, like, an art school . . . Like a rap thing.

AL: Well, did he use it in the context of the Beat writers or the Beat Generation?

JERRY: Well, somebody asked, "What is that?" And he just sort of said, "You're it, the Beat Generation."

AL: See, originally they used the word "Beat" like Kerouac.

JERRY: Right.

AL: Because it was an expression: "Man, I'm beat."

JERRY: Right, right. That kind of beat. This was a long time ago. But that stuff had enormous influences on me. I mean, I don't remember exactly what it was that brought that thing to my consciousness. But at first, it was just something, and later on it became something that I felt personally involved in, just because of that thing with being in art school, you know what I mean? With all the famous San Francisco painters, you know. And at that time The Place [a Beat bar] was happening down in . . .

AL: Grant Street. [Actually, Grant Avenue.]

JERRY: Yeah, Grant Street and all that stuff. You know, that's when I first fell into those kinds of scenes and started going to those places and hanging out as a kid.

DENNIS: What year was that? Do you recall?
JERRY: I was about fifteen, sixteen.

DENNIS: Yeah, because I always thought it was an incredible coincidence you picked up the guitar when you were fifteen.
JERRY: Uh huh.

DENNIS: And that was the year Kerouac's book [*On the Road*] came out, that fall, that October [actually September].
JERRY: Yeah, I read that. I mean, that was a major influence, that book, for everybody I knew.

AL: Well, did you pick up the guitar before or after you read that book?
JERRY: Oh, I played guitar before, because music and me is a whole life thing.

AL: Right.
JERRY: And that was, like, something else. That was like, you know, waking up and a whole other thing.

AL: What year was it, then, that you first started going up to North Beach?
JERRY: Let's see, it was right around when I got my first guitar, as a matter of fact. In fact, the reason I got my first guitar was that same teacher, Wally Hedrick, played acoustical guitar, and he brought a record of Big Bill Broonzy and his acoustical guitar to one of our classes. He also played banjo, four-string banjo, in one of the jazz bands around San Francisco. Traditional jazz. And I heard him play the guitar, and I heard Big Bill Broonzy on this record, and that's when I really decided, you know, I definitely do want a guitar. I had been wanting one, you know,

Emerald City.
Mixed media on paper.

behind listening to rock 'n' roll and all that stuff, and that was like what really pushed me over.

》》》　《《《

JERRY: At that time, the kind of stuff I was doing was playing the piano and singing, that kind of stuff. I wasn't playing. That wasn't what I did. I was just a kid.

AL: Well, you were playing at home.

JERRY: Yeah, but I didn't. When I finally got into the guitar and all that stuff, all my art trip, just … it went away. Everything went away.

FRIEND: How did that happen?

JERRY: I wanted a guitar. And on my fifteenth birthday, my mother got me an accordion. [*laughing quietly*]

FRIEND: Far out.

JERRY: This accordion, it was beautiful, and it was really far out. I guess she thought I wanted it or something, but I was upset about it because I wanted this electric guitar that was down in a pawnshop. So I traded the accordion for the electric guitar.

AL: Fifteen.

DENNIS: So you pretty much lost interest in art?

JERRY: Well, I did, I really tried, I made an effort. You know, I really made an effort, because I was an amateur guitarist, right? I wasn't taking lessons or anything like that. I only knew a few little fundamental minor things, but I just found myself playing the guitar all the time. You know, I would just get up in the morning and pick up the guitar and play it, you know. And you know, when I got my hands on it, it just seemed like that was all I was doing. And I didn't really flash on that until later, until after I got out of the army, actually.

》》》 《《《

JERRY: When I started playing the guitar, believe me, I didn't know anybody that played. I mean, I didn't know anybody that played the guitar. Nobody. They weren't around. There were no guitar teachers. You couldn't take lessons. There was nothing like that, you know? When I was a kid and I had my first electric guitar, I had it tuned wrong and learned how to play on it with it tuned wrong for about a year. And I was getting somewhere on it, you know … Finally, I met a guy that knew how to tune it right and showed me three chords, and it was like a revelation. You know what I mean? It was like somebody gave me the key to heaven. [laughs] I swear, you know?

DENNIS: I know. I can't even imagine.
JERRY: I was so hungry to play, man.

DENNIS: You must have been incredibly hungry to keep going for a year before, you know, you get those …
JERRY: I had to do it, man. I had to make that sound. You know? Man, I'm telling you. It was like a disease with me. It took me over, it really did.

DENNIS: How much, nowadays, do you tend to …
JERRY: There it is, you know [gesturing to his practice guitar and setup]. There it is.

DENNIS: Yeah.
JERRY: Here's my little Rockman practice amp, right here. Here's my books down here. I'm working now on fourths. You know, I've got a bunch of exercises here. In the middle of the night is when I'm happening, you know. Like, about two or three in the morning, I break this sucker out and then I play it, and I look up and it's six, you know? Five or six.

I don't know how long I do it, and sometimes I do one little thing over and over and over and over again, and it's one of those things, it gets me, you know.

DENNIS: Uh huh.

JERRY: But I don't feel very comfortable if it isn't about that far, that close to me most of the time, you know?

>>> <<<

> "I had to do it, man. I had to make that sound. You know? Man, I'm telling you. It was like a disease with me."

JERRY: Well, my mother, in a last attempt to pull me out of this trip, because I was into drugs and all this stuff . . . we moved, finally, out into the country, Northern California, out into Cazadero, which is up at the end of the Russian River. And really remote. I rode sixty miles [twenty-five each way] to school.

AL: That's when you get to Sebastopol.

JERRY: Yeah, Sebastopol School [Analy High School].

FRIEND: How old were you then?

JERRY: I was sixteen. No, seventeen.

FRIEND: She made that move just for you?

JERRY: Yeah.

FRIEND: Really?

JERRY: Well, you know, that, and she wanted to get out of the city and all that.

>>> <<<

While at Analy High School, Jerry met Gary Foster and joined his first band.

DENNIS: Gary Foster—

JERRY: Yeah.

DENNIS: —was saying that—
JERRY: He's a sweet guy.

DENNIS: Very nice guy.
JERRY: He was like one of the few guys that befriended me when I moved up to
Sebastopol.

DENNIS: Do you remember the name of the band you were in with him?
JERRY: No, I don't.

DENNIS: The Chords.
JERRY: The Chords?

DENNIS: The Chords.
JERRY: Incredible.

DENNIS: The very fact that you could play without music in front of you so
impressed him that he—
JERRY: Well, the very fact that he could play with music in front of him impressed me.

DENNIS: Impressed you, right. It was mutual.
JERRY: I was a total ignoramus then. I mean, I could play in, like, two or three keys
and up until that point I had had no exposure to other musicians except for
my cousin Danny, who taught me virtually everything I knew, such as it was.
I mean, if it wasn't for him, I probably never would have gotten to the point
where I could play.

M. G.: Tell him about the guitar upside down, I remember you telling me?
JERRY: Not upside down, but I had a tuning, an open tuning for it. I played in that for
about a year before somebody straightened me out. Showed me how to tune
it right and that was really weird.

DENNIS: That was—"Oh wow."

JERRY: Then I had to relearn everything, you know?

DENNIS: As you say, slow, and constantly catching up.

JERRY: Slow, but steady. Not so steady even, but slow certainly.

DENNIS: Ugly, but honest. Well, ugly will do.

JERRY: Gary was really fun to play with. He was pretty game, you know? And he was patient enough to show me shit that I otherwise would never have picked up in a million years. I mean, those songs were not, you know, they weren't bebop or anything like that, but they were the kind of changes that I didn't start to understand until I was playing with Merl [Saunders] for a couple of years.

DENNIS: He said it was forties big band stuff.

JERRY: Yeah, I was flying blind, essentially. You know what I mean? And he would tell me what to play . . . He had to show me where to put my capo because I could only play with a capo in those days, because I could only play in the first position. And so he would work out the math, you know? And like, "Okay, we're playing in E flat. Put the capo here as though you were playing in C," you know? "Transpose for me." All that stuff was stuff I didn't understand. I mean, I didn't know what notes were. Where the notes were on the guitar. I barely knew the names of the chords I could play. I was really ignorant, but I was into rock 'n' roll.

DENNIS: Right.

JERRY: So I could play pretty convincing rock 'n' roll, sort of, as long as it was, like, the blues fifties rock 'n' roll.

DENNIS: Right.

JERRY: Nothing more advanced than that, certainly. And even some of the songs threw me then. Some of them were even too complicated, but, you know, I just knew I loved it. That was all I knew.

DENNIS: Yeah. You had to wait for Ron Stevenson [a friend Jerry met in the army] to give you the graduation touches.

JERRY: Yeah. He didn't know much more than I did, but he knew just enough more than me where I could begin to see all kinds of stuff, and he could do a little bit of fingerpicking so I could—"Oh, I see," you know? That was the sound I heard on some records, solos like on some Elvis Presley records even.

Elvis Presley's guitarist, Scotty Moore, c. 1958.

84

DENNIS: Scotty Moore.

JERRY: Scotty Moore, right, played some things that he did a little bit of fingerpicking, Merle Travis style. I'd never heard Merle Travis. I'd never heard Chet Atkins. I'd never heard any of those guys. And I just thought I heard something that sounded cool as hell on those records. "What the fuck is that?" I tried to duplicate it, but it didn't seem possible. And then Ron Stevenson would play and he did just a little bit of fingerpicking and I said, "Oh, I see. You use your fingers!" That was a big revelation to me. It never even occurred to me to use my fingers. I mean, for me it was like, every little thing was like wow.

DENNIS: A revelation.

JERRY: Yeah.

>>> <<<

Jerry dropped out of Analy High School and joined the army. It was not a good fit; he prioritized friendship over obedience to army discipline, and missed a number of formations due to a crisis he talks about below. This led to him speaking with an army psychiatrist.

JERRY: The only shrink I've ever spoken to that was one of those situations where it really was a shrink and he really was doing his job—thinking he was doing his job—was when I was in the army. In fact, that guy gave me a nice bill of health. I was a total psychotic. I was, you know, "Garcia is a soft-spoken young man with a complete set of," you know, something. What was it he said? Oh, he felt that it was neurotic of me to have my own values. That was what it was.

DENNIS: Well. That's true.
JERRY: Yeah, right, it was. Especially if they were different from the army's.

DENNIS: If "neurotic" is not adjusted, and if you're in the army, right, it's neurotic to think for yourself. Of course it is.
JERRY: I told him that I was involved in stuff that was more important to me in the moment than the army was and that was the reason I was late. That was why I was fucking up.

DENNIS: Really. And they didn't understand.
JERRY: Well, a friend of mine [Ron Stevenson, who'd shown Jerry how to fingerpick guitar] was sitting in a hotel room. He was also AWOL. He was sitting in a hotel room threatening to kill himself. He'd recently married the sister of this girlfriend of mine at the time, and the family of this girl was begging me to go and get him to not kill himself, you know, and I had to do this instead of the army, you know what I mean? I mean, what would you do? So I told the guy, "Hey, that's what I had to do," you know what I mean? To me it was more important than the army. I was late for the army, but you know, hey, so I missed a couple of days of army. That was why. Anyway, that was it. So that made me crazy, and they gave me a general discharge and that's how I got out of the army.

DENNIS: God bless 'em.

JERRY: Yeah. Right. It was very nice of them, actually. It worked out great. I got out just as it was getting dull. Really. I had great fun while I was in the army. No kidding. All the time I was in there. It was really a kick. It was just different enough for a seventeen-year-old, you know what I mean.

DENNIS: Yeah.

JERRY: And just weird enough, just enough weird new stuff, just enough bullshit and that kind of stuff going on, and I was in it just to the point where it started to get to be really boring, which is finally what it does. It finally gets boring.

DENNIS: Oh, yeah.

**Boaz from *Sirens of Titan*.
Pen and ink on paper.**

JERRY: And then that happened and I got kicked out. It wasn't a moment too soon.

DENNIS: And the irony is you got the cake assignment in the entire United States Army.

JERRY: Tell me about it, man. I was in the headquarters company at Fort Winfield Scott [at the Presidio in San Francisco]. You know what I mean? It was the softest, the juiciest ... It was the best. Guys had maneuvered for years ... That's why I got out so easy. The last thing my company commander wanted was a troublemaker. Good heavens, somebody to make waves. Never, no. The first thing is, "You want to get out? Right away." No waves.

DENNIS: "We can accommodate."

JERRY: "No waves, you're out." That place was incredible. Man, there were maybe thirty of us there and it was a company [ordinarily a company has between 80 and 250 members]. You know? So I mean, they got the rations for a whole fuckin' company. There were guys black marketing. I sat up all night with the armorer filing serial numbers off of .45s and he'd take them out and sell them. It was incredible. There were guys skimming in every way. The army, you know.

Big Shoes. Mixed media on paper.

DENNIS: Somebody told me about you driving out to Point Bonita with a garbage truck. You got the weirdest duty in the whole world.

JERRY: Oh, yeah. I used to drive those three-quarter-ton, deuce-and-a-halves, to make the garbage run out to Fort Cronkhite [in the Marin Headlands] there. Then I drove a five-ton wrecker.

DENNIS: You're kidding.

JERRY: No kidding. And I worked on missiles. I worked on guided missiles.

DENNIS: Doesn't that make you feel really confident in the United States Army?

JERRY: Oh, well—

DENNIS: Jerry Garcia—

JERRY: They didn't work then. Why should they work now?

DENNIS: I don't know.

JERRY: The whole thing was so illuminating. You know what I mean? First of all, the thing of finding out the military … how incredibly incompetent it is. There is that saying they have in the army about the unwilling.

DENNIS: Yeah. Leading the incompetent, run by the …
JERRY: To do the unnecessary.

DENNIS: The unnecessary in an unbelievable amount of time.
JERRY: Right, all that stuff. It's all so true.

DENNIS: See, I've got the weirdest point of view on that because my father was in the army, but he was a spy.
JERRY: Oh, incredible.

DENNIS: Oh, it was the whole trip, and he was a very, very bright guy who never made it past, I think, it was E6—like a low-level sergeant—basically because he couldn't deal with the authority, you know? He could not politic.
JERRY: A lot of guys in the army like that. Yeah. Guys that couldn't take any amount of bullshit. And the military is a perfect place to hide out for them. I met some amazing guys. I met those kind of guys that were running away from three wives, you know, and guys with incredible scams. It was really amazing.

DENNIS: It's a kind of structure where the scam-minded can find the … you know? It's so big that you can find your little crevice …

JERRY: Right. There are guys in the army that really couldn't survive anyplace else, and there are guys in there that are taking advantage … The ultimate in escapist lives, you know what I mean?

DENNIS: Once you sign the line, you don't have to make another decision for the rest of your life.
JERRY: Really. Right. Oh, man, tell me about it. I met guys who had that down to an art, the art of not making a decision, of being a career non-decision-maker.

DENNIS: A career … Oh, God.

JERRY: Really. That was a wonderful experience, you know? I really lucked out when I got assigned to that place because it really was the cream … Everybody who was there wanted to be there.

DENNIS: Yeah.

JERRY: Except for maybe one or two of us who lucked out.

DENNIS: Accidents.

JERRY: The rest of them were guys who had jockeyed and fuckin' maneuvered to get there, you know?

DENNIS: You did your basic at Ord? [Fort Ord, in Seaside, California.]

JERRY: Yeah.

DENNIS: The usual hoo-ha.

JERRY: Right.

DENNIS: Yeah, that's funny.

JERRY: It was.

DENNIS: That's funny.

JERRY: My army career, what a joke.

DENNIS: Yeah.

JERRY: I was so earnest, too. You know? I was a seventeen-year-old. I mean, I really thought, "Well, here I'm going to join the army and go to fuckin' Germany or something. I'm going to get something out of this. I'm going to go somewhere, cut something loose." I didn't even get out of the state. It was incredible. I barely got out of San Francisco County, shit.

Jerry on Lenny Bruce

One of the recurring themes in Jerry's life was his great good fortune in connecting with artists and learning from them. This included both the painters he studied in art school, and early important musicians—Bill Monroe, for instance, and, later, bluegrass fiddler Scotty Stoneman. But his study of Lenny Bruce truly came out of left field, and he learned more than I think even he knew.

Jerry describes here the unusual circumstances that connected him with Bruce, who had been arrested for a so-called "obscene" routine. In order to defend himself in court, Lenny needed his own transcripts of his show, since the ones the cops and district attorneys were using were . . . not entirely reliable. Jerry had been deciphering lyrics on scratchy old recordings for a while. He had the ear, and Bruce's attorney hired him to transcribe the audio of his show. It would be an invaluable experience for him.

It's important to understand how significant Lenny Bruce really was. Comedy in the early '60s was starting to widen its range—Mort Sahl, for instance, was introducing sociopolitical material; Nichols and May were adding a level of sophisticated wit that was light-years beyond Bob Hope's funny but terribly conservative one-liners or Red Skelton's clowning. Further back, of course, the Marx Brothers had essentially strafed America with anarchist bombs, but even they performed behind a Hollywood veil that concealed their mad message.

Lenny Bruce was something else. Lenny was *dangerous*. Having come of professional age in the 1950s, he paralleled the Beats by dipping into jazz improvisation and spontaneity to broach subjects like sex, patriotism, religion, race, and drugs—and after that he got controversial. He honed his act—really, it wasn't exactly an act, it was a mind revealing itself—at San Francisco's own hungry i, and it was in San Francisco that he was first arrested for obscenity, after a set at the Jazz Workshop on October 4, 1961. "Obscenity, who really cares / Propaganda, all is phony," sang Dylan just four years later. Lenny had used some words that probably don't fly in so-called "polite" company, but it was the implications of his ruminations on the Roman Catholic Church in his famous "Father Flotsky" routine that set the Irish Catholic district attorneys of America on his trail. So the vice squad began attending every show, and it was their version of his show that was presented to juries. "They're doing my act," said Lenny. "And they stink." In transcribing the tapes, Jerry got to listen to and study Lenny up close, gaining lessons in language, style, and social criticism that no other nineteen-year-old in America could imagine.

The conversation began with how Jerry got the job transcribing Lenny Bruce tapes.

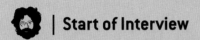 ## | Start of Interview

JERRY: The two Edmiston brothers, Joe Edmiston [the Edmiston brothers were bandmates of Jerry's in a old-time music group called the Thunder Mountain Tub Thumpers], his wife, Marilyn Mumford, a friend of one of my grade school chums, was working as Lenny Bruce's secretary during the time when Lenny Bruce was going through all his trials, so he had to have transcripts of his tapes for their trials for the dirty words. You know?

DENNIS: Oh, yeah.

JERRY: So I had a job working for a little while.

DENNIS: So you knew how to type?

JERRY: No. I don't know how to type. I had to do it longhand. The thing was, the reason I was good at it was because I spent a lot of time listening to old-time records and was able to pick . . .

DENNIS: You had a good ear.

JERRY: To hear indecipherable voices and tell what the words were. You know? I had an ear for it.

DENNIS: And he'd be tough.

JERRY: And he had the thing of mumbling a paragraph, but it was a real paragraph, you know? He had a shorthand way of talking when he was mumbling, like a speed freak.

DENNIS: Uh huh.

JERRY: But it was real content. You know? It was real stuff, and so you had to . . . you know?

DENNIS: Yeah. Actually, you'd be ideal for it.

JERRY: It was incredible. I learned so much.

DENNIS: What a wonderful . . .

JERRY: It was. It blew my mind. I learned so much.

DENNIS: You get paid to really listen to a master.

JERRY: Yeah. It was a trip. It was a trip. I only had a little bit. But, you know, that's why I know about transcribing, because that was a nightmare and I had to do things like go to the library . . . He used to do a bit where he'd take a magazine, a newspaper, a magazine, current, like a *Newsweek* or something. He'd thumb through it while he was onstage and he'd thumb through it and he'd look at things and then he'd riff off of some article. And what I would have to do is listen to what he was saying as he was thumbing through it and then I would have to go and look for the *Newsweek* he had.

DENNIS: Uh huh.

JERRY: Behind what he mumbled as he was going past, and he would read a little and [*imitating Bruce mumbling*]. You know?

DENNIS: What a neat like level of research.

JERRY: It was incredible. I had to go and get things to tell what he was talking about because some of the things were so off the wall and I didn't understand. And all of a sudden, he would break into this weird thing and I'd go and find the article. It would be something in chemistry or science or, you know, religion or some weird thing. He'd see a paragraph that would jump out at him and all of a sudden start riffing. It was fascinating, man. I mean really. But he had that wonderful thing of being able to . . . he was like a speed reader or something. He could condense. I swear to God, he could condense all the key stuff in, like, three or four paragraphs. You know? And say it in this kind of fast mumble. It would be a mumble that represented maybe seven syllables. You know? But it had little bits and pieces of everything in the article. It was incredible. I learned a lot about linguistics listening to him do that because he did a thing with a speech that was like Neal [Cassady] did, and it had some subtle levels to it. It was like bebop language. You know? It really was. He'd take bits and pieces of language and it was totally unselfconscious, you know what I mean? I'm sure he didn't know that he was doing it.

DENNIS: Yeah.
JERRY: But he was just rapping.

4

The Slingshot

Early in 1961, Jerry gratefully exited the army and settled in East Palo Alto, the poor side of town. Palo Alto was much warmer than San Francisco, a good place for a guy who was known to sleep in his car. Even then he had charm and a (now acoustic) guitar, which led to a number of free meals courtesy of some female Stanford students. His life revolved around a coffeehouse called Saint Michael's Alley, Kepler's Books, and the folk music clubs that were beginning to pop up all over the Bay Area. In short order, he became friends with a number of guys who'd become a permanent part of his life, including a musician and proto-novelist named Robert Hunter, a visiting English student named Alan Trist, and an eccentric thinker named Willy Legate. There was also a budding artist named Paul Speegle, son of the drama critic of the *San Francisco News-Call Bulletin*. Late in February, Jerry, Alan, Paul, and two others were in a terrible car accident that killed Paul and changed Garcia's life forever, giving it a new purposefulness as he grappled with his very narrow escape from death.

His adult life had begun. He applied himself to his guitar and fairly soon became proficient in playing old-time acoustic music, part of the purist wing of the folk music scene that had swept America after the demise of '50s rock (Elvis in the army, Chuck Berry in jail, Little Richard retired to the ministry). Soon he picked up the banjo, and plunged into the slightly maniacal world of bluegrass. On occasion, he would enjoy himself with a pickup gig on bass for a rock band called the Zodiacs, which he talks about here. The year 1964 brought the British Invasion—first the Beatles, then many others, and soon the Rolling Stones; Jerry had a friend, a blues-soaked harmonica player most frequently known as Pigpen, who told him that they, too, could play electric blues, and Jerry was convinced. So the Warlocks were born. They began playing in public in 1965, a rich year for Garcia, one full of experiences that would, forever after, feed his life.

The first revelation came in April, when a friend of his showed up with a baggie full of a substance that would open the doors of perception for him: LSD. Along with music, it would be one of the fundamental influences of his life. Another of the great encounters of 1965 was hearing Bob Dylan for the first time. As a purist old-time music folkie, Garcia had previously paid little attention to Dylan, who didn't quite fit Jerry's standards ("I can be a terrible puritan," he confessed).

He talks eloquently about the music of this era—the Byrds' version of "Mr. Tambourine Man," "Satisfaction," and "Like a Rolling Stone" were the summer's number-one songs, a pretty remarkable level of quality in the world of Top 40 music— and the emergence of what came to be called folk rock, as more and more folkies followed the Beatles' lead and picked up electric instruments. The Warlocks were part of a giant wave responding to the British Invasion, and this is made clear in two stories Jerry tells. One is of seeing the Lovin' Spoonful, led by his acquaintance John Sebastian, a veteran of the Even Dozen Jug Band along with Jerry's friend David Grisman, just as Jerry had been part of Mother McCree's Uptown Jug Champions. The second story recounts how Jerry ran into his folkie pal Jorma Kaukonen at a bluegrass show in San Jose in August and learned that Jorma, too, was now part of a rock band—Jefferson Airplane.

This chapter ends with the Warlocks' jaunt to their first adult rock dance, at Longshoreman's Hall in San Francisco. Put on by a group of friends called the Family Dog, it would point to the future—and the Warlocks' part in that.

 | Start of Interview

JERRY: When they slipped me out of the Permanente Hospital, you know, I just—all I wanted to do was get away from there before I had to pay something. And they also wouldn't give me a painkiller, those motherfuckers. I laid on a slab all night long, moaning and groaning. I mean, really. It hurt so bad. You know? Oh, God.

97

DENNIS: Yeah.
JERRY: Ah, shit. Moaning and groaning, my face covered with blood, you know, and I just hurt so bad, I didn't know what . . . I was groaning and moaning.

DENNIS: They wouldn't even—
JERRY: They wouldn't give me nothing. No one even came in to look at me, you know? Fuck. It was horrible. And finally early in the morning they stuck me in an ambulance and sent me over to the Permanente Clinic in San Mateo where they ran me through an X-ray to see if there was anything horribly smashed or something. That was the first they got around to X-raying me.

DENNIS: Uh huh.
JERRY: And they didn't find anything that bad, and I had some friends who were there and they just took me home. They took me to where I was staying and I just piled up on the couch there and lay there for a few days and that was it.

I found where they towed the car to. It looked like a crumbled pack of cigarettes. It was nothing.

DENNIS: Where you physically landed.

JERRY: It had dirt impacted into the, you know, the top of the windows? You know, the roof? Here's the ceiling and the inside of the ceiling in the car. Here's the window. There was dirt and sod impacted into the space between the window and the roof. You know, dirt is jammed in there in the—

DENNIS: It's weird. It rolled?

JERRY: It must have gone flying end over end, you know? I don't know what happened.

DENNIS: You were thrown, right?

Volkswagen Abduction.
Pen and ink on paper.

JERRY: I went through the windshield. Yeah.

DENNIS: I knew you were lucky to get out of that one, but I didn't realize it was that lucky.

JERRY: Yeah, I went through the windshield. It was so violent and so furious that I don't even know. I have no ... nothing. You know, for me there was an unbroken moment between being in the car and being in a field, and that's it. You know? There's nothing in between. I don't know what happened, really. That car just must have went flying. I mean, at ninety miles an hour, things happen fast.

DENNIS: It was like that, they were going that fast?

JERRY: Oh, yeah. We were hauling. We

The Orange Beetle.
Mixed media on paper.

were going fast. It was a Studebaker Golden Hawk, you know, with a blower in it. They went fast.

DENNIS: Street machine. Yeah. Amazing.

JERRY: It was the only car that came stocked with a blower.

DENNIS: Right. Yeah that's—

JERRY: Horsepower city, but zero suspension. It hit those chatter bars, you know, in the divider.

DENNIS: Right. It just ripped the wheel out of [driver Lee Adams's] hands—

JERRY: The instant it hit them, it must have just went flying.

DENNIS: Right.

JERRY: It was incredible. I guess. I don't know what happened. I really don't know.

DENNIS: Did you find your shoes?

JERRY: Yeah. My shoes were in the car under the seat.

DENNIS: Talk about being blown out of your shoes.

JERRY: That's right. I was literally thrown out of my shoes. That's what the force of it was like. It was a sobering sensation.

DENNIS: Yeah. I guess. I guess.

JERRY: I was amazed. And when I saw what that car looked like, believe me, I was so amazed I was alive. I couldn't believe it. That thing was a total loss. It was just . . . it looked like a smashed beer can or anything, you know what I mean? It was junk. The violence must have been incredible.

DENNIS: Yeah. Yeah. Jesus.

JERRY: My life started there.

>>> <<<

JERRY: I was fucking around until there really. I was just a dumb kid. I mean, I had a few half-formed ideas, but my life—that is the slingshot, *boom*, you know? That's what got me going. That's what gave life that urgency, you know? That was hard. That stuff is hard when you're young. The grief. When you lose a brother, when you lose a pal.

DENNIS: I lost family, but—
JERRY: So did I. That's why I was so used to it in a certain way, but this was something new to me, the thing of losing a comrade. He was, like, a new friend, too. It was like we were just getting chummy. We were just getting really fond of each other, you know? And you know how it is when you're young and there's that excitement.

DENNIS: Yeah. And that has not happened to me yet. Don't say that out loud.
JERRY: Yeah. Right.

DENNIS: Yeah, you know, I called his father.
JERRY: Yeah.

DENNIS: And just explained who I was and said a lot of people—you know, "Just for what it's worth, a lot of people in this scene really, very much strongly remember Paul and all that and I'd like to know a little more about him. Could I come talk to you some time?"
JERRY: I bet it was painful for him.

DENNIS: He said yes, and when I called to make the appointment he said, you know, "I just can't do it." I said, I completely understand. It's cool.
JERRY: He seemed so small and frail and sad. I used to read his column, too.

101

"That stuff is hard when you're young. The grief. When you lose a brother, when you lose a pal."

DENNIS: Right.

JERRY: A well-known guy.

DENNIS: Mr. McKernan was the same way, and it was like, hey, understood.

JERRY: I know how those guys feel. It's hard for those guys to be men in those days, you know what I mean? They had so much bullshit and they got hurt more and didn't have any place to show it.

DENNIS: Yeah.

JERRY: They didn't have any place to put it, you know?

>>> <<<

Equipped with a new seriousness, Jerry became a devoted player of acoustic music, especially the bluegrass banjo. But occasionally he played bass in the Zodiacs, a rock band led by Troy Weidenheimer.

JERRY: Troy was a lot of fun, but I wasn't good enough a musician then to have been able to deal with it. I was out of my idiom, really, 'cause when I played with Troy I was playing electric bass, you know. I never was a good bass player. Sometimes I was playing in the wrong key and didn't even fuckin' know it. I couldn't hear that low, after playing banjo, you know, and going to electric.

DENNIS: Really. "I hear high."

JERRY: But Troy taught me the principle of, hey, you know, just stomp your foot and get on it. He was great. A great one for the instant arrangement, you know. And he was also fearless for that thing of get your friends to do it. Fuck it if it ain't slick.

DENNIS: It's supposed to be fun. If it ain't fun, it ain't worth it.

JERRY: He was good at that. And he was also a very good player, too. And I admired him. He was facile. And, he had a great sense of humor, too. He was a funny guy. He was a lot of fun to hang out with.

>>> <<<

Finally came 1965, a year of wonders for Garcia. One of the greatest events of his life was his first experience with LSD.

DENNIS: Interestingly enough, at almost this exact time, while helping your current chief economic officer, Ms. B. Parker, and her then husband to move, you did your first acid trip.

JERRY: That's right. That's exactly right.

DENNIS: You got any specific memories of that first trip?

JERRY: [*laughter*] Well, where should I start?

DENNIS: Outside of Nelson bringing home winos and … [David Nelson was a close friend of Garcia's—he had been the best man at Jerry's wedding to Sara Ruppenthal—who played guitar in several of Jerry's early-sixties acoustic bands and later in the New Riders of the Purple Sage.]

JERRY: I remember walking around for a long time with Butch Waller. He was dumping the furniture from his life, you know, and he says, "That's just bullshit," and I was dumping the furniture from my life. And then I had a desire to go and see Sara. I said, "Hey, I got to take my old lady along with this." So I got a cap, took it home to go and get high. And then we all just ran around the streets for the rest of the night. I mostly worried, you know, because I thought … I always have that thing of worry, you know? I guess I worried about myself, so I'd always project it on whoever I thought might be weak.

DENNIS: Right.

JERRY: Somebody's going to freak out; who's going to freak out? I went through a certain amount of that. But mostly it was that wonderful feeling you get when … it's like, suspicions confirmed, you know?

DENNIS: I did my first acid trip at a Grateful Dead concert.

JERRY: I had a perfectly wonderful time, and it was that soft psychedelia, you know,

103

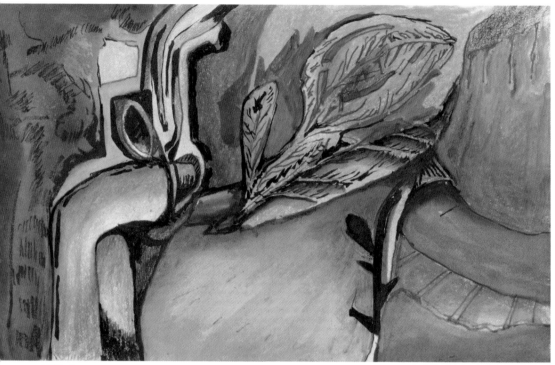

Acid Peach.
Pastel and pen on paper.

the first thing, the first stuff. It was very soft and sweet and great fun. It wasn't particularly miraculous. It was just that thing of solving all earthly problems.

DENNIS: Just that incredible flash, "My God, there is a whole lot more going on . . ."

JERRY: Right. And all the stuff that I've been dealing with has been mostly bullshit, but at least I knew that there was something else and I'm glad I was right. So I felt pretty good, really. That was what I came away with. And I felt exactly like continuing with doing exactly what I was doing and doing it more and better. You know, that's what I came away from. Tremendous affirmation and reassurance.

DENNIS: Yeah, I did it with you guys the first time.

JERRY: Out of sight.

》》》 《《《

JERRY: Then we went through a long period of time when we were taking LSD
during the days, and then just going off into the hills and romping and
getting crazy. That kind of stuff. That was a lot of fun. It was a long time,
and then we would be coming down and going to work. [The Warlocks
had a residency at the In Room in Burlingame.] You know, we'd go to work
at the bar, smoke pot, you know, during the night, and play our sets and
have the acid flashes. By that time the bar was almost completely empty of
customers. I guess you've heard by now that we drove every customer out of
the fuckin' place. The bartenders loved us and we turned them on.

DENNIS: It was interesting, because I had a certain notion of that bar. And God bless
him, Paul Grushkin [another Grateful Dead fan and researcher] dug up the
owner of that bar for me.

JERRY: Fantastic.

DENNIS: And it was like a mover's bar, you know? I mean, it was a hard liquor bar. It
was no college beer bar or something. It was like—

JERRY: A peninsula divorcées bar,
man.

DENNIS: Yeah, yeah, exactly. Okay,
now I understand what [you]
meant about driving them
out.

JERRY: They couldn't bullshit the
chicks with that racket
going on.

DENNIS: Dig it. You cannot pick up
when you're grinding away
on "Baby Blue" or whatever.

JERRY: Absolutely not. Also, by

The Warlocks, 1965.

then we had a reputation, too, in the clubs. We were, by then, well known in the clubs amongst the other club bands, the pros, you know, the bar bands. The guys that played in bars like we played in—the lifers. You know what I mean? The guys that were professionals. And we were getting a reputation for being the first guys to know the new Rolling Stones tunes, you know?

DENNIS: Yeah?

JERRY: Yeah. That was, like, the only concession we made to the thing—we got to play the hits, you know, we did Rolling Stones tunes.

DENNIS: Well, you also did a couple of Spoonful tunes.

JERRY: That's true, but that's about it.

The Green Machine.
Mixed media on paper.

DENNIS: Right.

JERRY: Everything else was just the stuff that we liked. You know?

DENNIS: Right.

JERRY: Weird R&B shit.

DENNIS: Yeah.

JERRY: That's right. And so, you know, we were getting into that head. We were getting in that space as far as developing a reputation and sort of being the Rolling Stones of the peninsula bar bands.

⟩⟩⟩ ⟨⟨⟨

DENNIS: You have said a number of times that the first time you had any particular interest in Dylan was *Bringing It All Back Home.*

JERRY: That's right.

DENNIS: That came out in April of 1965. [Actually, March 22.]
JERRY: Uh huh.

DENNIS: As a historian, '65 is an incredible fuckin' [year]. April '65, the Warlocks are playing for the first time. [There was possibly a first show at Menlo College preceding the May shows at Magoo's Pizza Parlor, which are generally thought to be the first Warlocks shows.]
JERRY: Yeah.

DENNIS: You do your first acid.
JERRY: Yeah.

DENNIS: You listen to *Bringing It All Back Home.*
JERRY: Yeah, it was a good year.

DENNIS: Man, a lot of shit starts happening. All in that one month, all this stuff happens.
JERRY: Right, it all did.

DENNIS: Just out of curiosity, Dylan played at Berkeley Community Theatre on April 3, 1965.
JERRY: Yeah, I remember that.

DENNIS: You didn't go?
JERRY: No, I didn't go. We were working, actually, I think, or something like that. We might have been—

DENNIS: Might have been a Magoo's night. It's very possible you might have been at Magoo's. [Probably not.]
JERRY: If we weren't working, we were doing something that made it impossible for us to go. I know I couldn't go to that one for some reason.

DENNIS: But like –
JERRY: Phil might have gone to that, though.

DENNIS: You were interested in it at any . . .
JERRY: Oh, sure.

DENNIS: You were aware of it at that point.
JERRY: I knew he was in town and all that, yeah. But I was not a big fan of Dylan's then, you know? It took a little while for me to get into it. As a folkie, I found him reprehensible.

〉〉〉 〈〈〈

JERRY: I think the first time I heard *Bringing It All Back Home*, I went over to Eric Thompson's place, and him and his roommate and the people that he was living with, they had all sat up all night and had eaten morning glory seeds. Remember those?

108

DENNIS: Yeah.
JERRY: Morning glory seeds. And they were all weird as hell, you know—"Hey, what's happening you guys?" [*Jerry vocalizes an incoherent response.*] And on the record player was playing *Bringing It All Back Home*.

And I think, actually, I had seen Bob Dylan on *The Les Crane Show*, and he sang "It's All Over Now, Baby Blue." That was one of the tunes he sang with what's-his-name playing the second guitar, the guy with no fingers. [Bruce Langhorne.] Good guitar player. He's the guy that played all that pretty sort of Eastern-sounding stuff. The second guitar, that nice low second guitar line on that record.

DENNIS: Now I get to go back and listen to it again.
JERRY: Yeah, it's very pretty, especially "It's All Over Now, Baby Blue." And that's the tune that he played. Although he said he was going to play the one about, "Mama's in the basement mixing up the—"

DENNIS: "Subterranean Homesick Blues."
JERRY: Yeah, he said he was going to play that.

DENNIS: That was the first single, as a matter of fact.
JERRY: Yeah, that's right.

DENNIS: The one that broke.
JERRY: He mentioned that.

DENNIS: And then [he] goes and plays—
JERRY: And played "It's All Over Now, Baby Blue," and that, I thought that was just gorgeous, I thought it was really a lovely sounding song. Although I didn't really catch it on the TV, but then I recognized it from the record. And when I heard it, I played it over and over and over again since it sounded so great.

DENNIS: For my money, the two greatest rock 'n' roll [songs]—if you've got to pick two, you know, for what it's worth—are "Satisfaction" and "Like a Rolling Stone."
JERRY: Yeah.

109

DENNIS: And to think that they came out, one in May and one in June of [1965]—you know, at the same time.
JERRY: Did they really?

DENNIS: Yeah.
JERRY: I'll be damned. I thought "Satisfaction" came out earlier than, quite a lot earlier.

New York at Night.
Watercolor on paper.

DENNIS: Wait a minute. I take it back.

JERRY: "Satisfaction" came out a year before, I'm sure. [starts singing the opening riffs of "Satisfaction"]

DENNIS: Oh, no, no, no. Jerry, I'm right about this. June of '65, or maybe May of '65, but summer of '65.

JERRY: "Like a Rolling Stone" didn't come out until *Blonde on Blonde*, right?

DENNIS: Oh, no, no, no. "Like a Rolling Stone" was a single cut after *Bringing It All Back Home*, and then was put on—

JERRY: Was it on *Highway 66*?

DENNIS: *61*, yeah.

JERRY: Oh.

DENNIS: Yeah. And that came out in about June. I might even have it written—

JERRY: *Highway 61*, whatever.

DENNIS: They came out very, very close to each other.

JERRY: I guess you're right. Yeah, I guess you're right. They did come out close to each other.

DENNIS: That summer of '65.

JERRY: Yeah, you're right. "Like a Rolling Stone" is one of the best ever, you're right, and "Satisfaction," too, one of the best ever. Yeah, you're right.

DENNIS: And so that's the thing. And then in June, you—

JERRY: What a year.

DENNIS: —and Sara [Sara Ruppenthal Garcia, Jerry's first wife], you got the Warlocks going. It's still the Warlocks. You've played at Magoo's. You've added Phil. You're now playing in places like the Fireside.

First recording session with the Grateful Dead, at Golden State Recorders, 1965.

JERRY: Yeah.

DENNIS: And the Cinnamon A-Go-Go.
JERRY: Right, right. Oh, wow.

DENNIS: And in June, you and Eric and maybe other people and Sara went to see the Spoonful at Mother's [a nightclub in San Francisco].
JERRY: That's right, at Mother's; that's right. I had forgotten about that.

DENNIS: I just went over the other day to interview [Erik] Jacobsen, their producer and all that.
JERRY: Yeah.

Contact sheet of first recording session with the Grateful Dead, at Golden State Recorders, 1965.

DENNIS: It was interesting—the way Sara remembers it, it was like you weren't a
stranger. You knew, somehow you knew—

JERRY: John Sebastian, slightly. 'Cause he was friends with David Grisman and all
those guys.

DENNIS: Right.

JERRY: And he had been in the Even Dozen Jug Band. And Grisman had been in the
Even Dozen Jug Band, and I knew Grisman, and that was my connection
with them.

DENNIS: And, actually, Eric [Thompson] had been back—

JERRY: And Eric knew him real well. I think Eric knew him actually much better than I did. Yeah, 'cause he had been back in New York. He had gone back and made himself a fair-haired boy. That was the thing. See, the thing was to go to New York and be discovered, and I didn't have the patience to stick it out. But Eric, he stuck it out.

DENNIS: You took one look at New York when you were with Sandy [in the summer of 1964, Jerry and his friend Sandy Rothman took a bluegrass pilgrimage across the country that took them very briefly to New York City], and said, "We're going to Boston."

JERRY: Yeah. I couldn't hack it. No, it wasn't for me.

DENNIS: Well, after New York, you get to San Francisco and you find out New York is how tough a city can be.

JERRY: Yeah.

DENNIS: And San Francisco is the hippest small town in America.

JERRY: Definitely.

DENNIS: It's like all the positive stuff of the city—

JERRY: Absolutely. And they all ended up moving out anyway. They all came out. The New York guys, I met them when they came out here. That's really how I met them mostly. Except for Grisman. I met him in a parking lot in Pennsylvania at Sunset Park, a bluegrass park. We picked together. And he knew of me because my reputation had spread to the East Coast with my friends. And I was known by reputation really, you know?

DENNIS: Right.

JERRY: So I might as well have been there. But I couldn't have hacked it, I don't think. It was too ugly for me.

DENNIS: No. And just definitely the whole San Francisco scene, you know, couldn't have happened except in San Francisco.

JERRY: Well, it was so great. And those guys all wanted to be someplace better than New York, anyways. They all ended up coming out here.

DENNIS: Right.

JERRY: That was the best place. It was obviously the best place to be.

DENNIS: Do you recall having any particular opinion about the Spoonful thing?

JERRY: I wasn't that taken with them at Mother's, but I liked their music. I liked their stuff. I thought it had a really neat sound. But I wasn't crazed about it, I don't think, you know?

DENNIS: Yeah. The fact that you were, like, attuned to the Spoonful at that point is—

JERRY: Well, because they were part of the folk world and I knew them from the folk world. That's what I knew them from.

DENNIS: And you were sort of in parallel because you had done the same transformation to electric.

JERRY: That's right. We were really part of that other society. We were part of that other social world.

》》》 《《《

DENNIS: In late July [1965], you've got Dylan going electric at Newport—a phenomenal moment. In August—on August 7th, the Mime Troupe was busted in the park, which ultimately led to all the benefits, and Bill and all that trip. The same day, the Hell's Angels did their first run to La Honda and to Kesey's place. Then in the middle of the month, the Jefferson Airplane debuted with the opening of the Matrix.

JERRY: Wow.

DENNIS: And the last day of the month, the Beatles played at the Cow Palace.

JERRY: Ah, far out. That was a busy month. That was a hell of a month.

114

DENNIS: Yeah, it was a very busy little month. Obviously, you didn't go to the Beatles shows.

JERRY: No, no, no.

"And those guys all wanted to be someplace better than New York, anyways. They all ended up coming out here."

DENNIS: Or pay any attention to any of those specifics, and at the same time, by about September— somewhere around September, is my best guess—you went into the In Room, so you were operating on that level.

JERRY: That's right. We were working around then, and we knew about the Beatles going into the—

DENNIS: Cow Palace. I think Bobby went.

JERRY: Somebody did from our scene.

DENNIS: I guess it was Weir.

JERRY: And Sue, of course. [Sue Swanson, Connie Bonner, and Bob Matthews were high school classmates of Bob Weir's and were the first fans of the Warlocks, the first Dead Heads.]

DENNIS: Sue Swanson, and—

JERRY: Sue and Bonny.

DENNIS: And who is the other girl?

JERRY: Connie Bonner.

DENNIS: Connie Bonner, right. Connie and Sue, of course, were the ultimo Beatle freaks.

JERRY: Rabid.

DENNIS: And they dragged Bobby. And he ended up, like, on the outside waiting for the—

JERRY: That's right, and the Pranksters went, too.

DENNIS: And the Pranksters went, and got blown out of their socks.
JERRY: Right, right.

DENNIS: They were not ready to rock 'n' roll.
JERRY: Right. Kesey couldn't get over it. Kesey lost it behind it.

DENNIS: So you're sort of hearing about all of that.
JERRY: Yeah, right. That was all in the air.

DENNIS: You had obviously known Kantner [Paul Kantner, cofounder of Jefferson Airplane] from just around—
JERRY: Sure.

116 **DENNIS:** —the Offstage and whatnot for quite a while. It seems to me I remember a bit where you talk about running into I think it was Jorma at this point, and him saying, "Oh, I'm in an electric band," and you saying, "Oh, far out, so am I."
JERRY: Yeah, I ran into him down at the In Room—not the In Room, the Offstage, which was just going into its tailspin decline then because Paul Foster was becoming a Prankster, freaking out good and solid.

DENNIS: Good and solid.
JERRY: Yeah. And I ran into him—I ran into Jorma, and it turned out he was in the Jefferson Airplane. It was funny. Yeah, I told him I was in an electric band. And I think the occasion was I went to see Dave Nelson playing with that band—that slick bluegrass band with Herb Pedersen in it, and Richard Greene was in it, too, at that time. And they were happening pretty good. They were in a good space.

DENNIS: Would that have been the Dillards or—
JERRY: No, no. They were—what the hell were they called? [The Pine Valley Boys.]

Author Ken Kesey (on the roof with hat and flute) and members of The Merry Pranksters onboard
the "Further" bus in New York City, June 1964.

DENNIS: David, at this time, was in the New Delhi River Band.

JERRY: Herb Pedersen, Butch Waller, Nelson was playing guitar for them briefly, and Richard Greene was playing fiddle. They put out one record on Elektra. I forget what the hell the name was. They were Bay Area. They weren't that good, really, but they were okay. No, they weren't even okay. I didn't think they were very good, but my friend David was in it. David was good, and Richard Greene was good. And they sang pretty good—Herb Pedersen was a hell of a singer.

DENNIS: Herb has a hell of a voice.

JERRY: Yeah. He was a sweet singer. I remember going down there to whatever club that was and running into Jorma there.

DENNIS: So that was your first flash of the Airplane.

JERRY: That's the first I think I heard of it, yeah. But I didn't realize that it was people I knew. I didn't realize it was Kantner and stuff. I didn't know Kantner, except that I did know him. I didn't know him by name, I just knew him because I had seen him zillions of times. I've seen him around for years.

DENNIS: Right.

JERRY: I just didn't know him personally really. I knew Jorma, and I knew David Freiberg slightly from David and Michaela [a Bay Area folk music duo]. He was a folkie. I mean, you know, it was all the same. So essentially the rock 'n' roll scene in San Francisco was the same old scene.

DENNIS: Exactly, exactly. Well, to me, you see, that's the ultimate.

JERRY: That's what I loved about it. That's what's hard to communicate to other people. You know what I mean?

DENNIS: For me, the essential fact of every one of those [bands]—the Quicksilver, Big Brother, the Airplane, and the Dead is that it's former folkies going electric.

JERRY: That's right. And we're all people that knew each other. At least some, you know. I mean, we all had more than a nodding acquaintance. We all bought dope from the same guys. Everybody smoked pot.

》》》 《《《

In the Fall of 1965, a group of people who'd spent the summer hanging out and doing LSD with a San Francisco band called the Charlatans at a place called the Red Dog Saloon in Virginia City, Nevada, dubbed themselves the Family Dog and began to hold dances at San Francisco's Longshoreman's Hall, the first local rock event for adults.

DENNIS: The classic comment is you guys farted around here on a nice Saturday afternoon—
JERRY: That's right.

DENNIS: —and bombed down to the Longshoreman's Hall.
JERRY: That's right.

DENNIS: So somehow you were aware of it in some fashion.
JERRY: Oh, sure, it was on the radio. They were running ads on the radio that sounded good. You know, it was—the names of them were good. It was like, "A Tribute to Dr. Strange" was the name of the dances, you know, and stuff like that. So we went to this one that was the Lovin' Spoonful and the Charlatans and somebody else maybe, and we went down. It was great. We were stoned on acid still, you know. We'd stopped at Clown Alley and got some burgers, living burgers you know? [When high on LSD, food is frequently

Facets 1.
Airbrush on paper.

"And Phil runs up to her, frothing at the mouth, and says, "Lady, what this little séance needs is us."

odd in appearance, hence "living" burgers.] And then we went to Longshoreman's Hall and stumbled in there. And Luria [Castell] was standing there, or Ellen [Harmon]. And Phil runs up to her, frothing at the mouth, and says, "Lady, what this little séance needs is us." You know, it's one of the greatest lines ever.

DENNIS: It is. There may have never been a better line for the moment . . .

JERRY: Blew my socks off. I cracked up. I really did. And I went inside and immediately ran into Chet Helms [a San Francisco hippie and marijuana legalization activist who would later take over the reins of Family Dog] who I didn't know from Adam, you know, and here's this hippie, you know, and he says, "This is great. Every hippie in town is here tonight in drag," and I thought, "Yeah, right you are. This is great. This is a hell of a trip. This is a lot of fun."

Dripping Graffiti.
Colored pens on paper.

Jerry on the Subject of LSD

Transcendence has been a human imperative as long as humans have been aware, but it's always been a tremendously difficult state to achieve. The meditative methods required extremely demanding discipline and rigor, and the various drugs humans have tried tasted awful and were wrenching to the body. Then in 1943, a Swiss research chemist looking for a drug that would encourage breathing but have no effect on the uterus synthesized something called lysergic acid diethylamide—LSD 25. It was so powerful that it required only the tiniest amounts and had almost no side effects. Few people would explore its possibilities more deeply than Jerry, the Warlocks (who became the Grateful Dead late in 1965), and their followers.

Though some might assume that Jerry would be an unabashed cheerleader for the use of psychedelics—and he certainly came down for the right of people to do so—he had a more nuanced point of view in this 1989 interview with journalist Jeremy Alderson. As was his way, he dismissed any claim to authority. In daily speech, he often punctuated a sophisticated and intelligent commentary on almost any given subject with the throwaway remark, "But what the fuck do I know?" It was one of the conundrums of Jerry Garcia: his intelligence, charm, and caring for other people added up to something I can only call charisma—people just naturally gravitated toward him.

But even as he unintentionally acquired "followers," Garcia consciously worked to deny responsibility for decisions. I once addressed him as "Boss," and someone objected. Jerry snickered and said, "Hey, he can call me boss. Just don't expect me to make any decisions." Another time, he was asked about his refusal to speak onstage, and replied that the great power of being literally above much of the audience with a sound system at his command suggested the potential for psychological fascism, particularly given an audience that was mostly high. Music, he felt, was pure; speech carried with it the potential for misleading and confusing people.

And so he acknowledged the risks of LSD, the possibility of people misusing it as a tool of domination (as the CIA tried, but failed, to do), and the inherent unpredictability of any LSD experience. He also offered some highly perceptive comments about what he perceived as the wider societal impact of LSD, how it may well have contributed to the recent evolution of scientific thinking from what he called "lab rat" determinism to the more subtle understanding evidenced in chaos studies and quantum physics. As usual, his main message was a refusal to make any conclusions, but to suggest the need for open-ended, intelligent study. Finally, at the end of this conversation, he shares with Jeremy Alderson details of his most extraordinary trip, an unforgettable day at Olompali (a house in Marin County where the Grateful Dead and friends lived) in the summer of 1966.

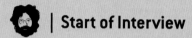 | **Start of Interview**

JERRY: These experiences, to me, I mean, the whole drug discussion is one of those things that I really don't feel qualified to advise anybody on any level of it, you know what I mean? I think it's really one of those things that everybody has to deal with, based on who they are and whatever, you know what I mean? So I feel a little funny talking about this stuff just because it's important and valuable to me, but I couldn't, I wouldn't recommend it to anybody else. Unless there was something in their life saying, do this, you know?

JEREMY: Well, it's okay not to share your experiences. I'm hoping people will get an idea about things just from the collective sense of what it really means to people.

JERRY: Yeah, well, for me it was a profoundly life-changing experience. It has a lot to do with where I am now and why I'm here and why I do what I do, and it all fits in and it was all happening as I was making the decisions to become who I am, you know what I mean? It all steered me directly into this place.

⟩⟩⟩ ⟨⟨⟨

Jeremy asks Jerry what his feelings about LSD are now, in 1989.

JERRY: Well, they haven't changed very much. My feelings about LSD are mixed. It's something that I fear and I love, also, at the same time. I never have a psychedelic experience without having that feeling of "I don't know what's going to happen," you know? In that sense, it's still fundamentally an enigma and a mystery. And there is no way I can predict what it's going to do. So in that sense, it's the way it was when I first had it. Even when I first heard about it. What is it? I don't know.

>>> <<<

JEREMY: Here's one. Is LSD a cure for what ails humanity?

JERRY: I don't think so. No. I don't even know whether it's helpful, but I think that for some people it's definitely a tool. So it may be useful in the aid of humanity. But on the other hand, I mean, you come up with Charlie Manson kind of people, you know what I mean? You come up with people who are psychedelic fascists and psychedelic rapists and psychedelic vampires. It's another thing that has a lot of power going along with it. And if you're unscrupulous enough, you could conceivably manipulate people using LSD. Certainly, the CIA tried to do it. Or at least according to the reports, they tried to do it.

JEREMY: Right.

JERRY: So that kind of stuff, I've seen it myself. That kind of pychedelic fascism, you know . . .

JEREMY: Mm-hmm.

JERRY: There is such a thing. And I don't think it always liberates people. I think that if you're looking to be liberated, it can help you. Certainly it can affirm your suspicions that there's more than just this. To me that is the most substantial thing, really. Whether you pay attention to what happens to you while you're having psychedelic experiences, I don't think is really the point. I think just the notion that the possibilities are much larger than normal perception lets you believe. You know, all of a sudden you have a lot more material. From an honest point of view, alone, whether you believe it or whether it has any context in which to stick it or anything, it's just lots of material. So just for the expanded point of view, that's going to be valuable to some kinds of people, I think. But anything with that much power going to it always has the downside, you know?

>>> <<<

One of the interesting effects of LSD, Jerry thought, was its wider social impact on scientific thinking in general.

JERRY: That's all. I mean, not enough is known. There have been a few people who have put forward some good models about how some psychedelics work, the McKenna brothers [Terence and Dennis McKenna were noted researchers in the area of psychedelic experience] and so forth, and some other researchers and stuff. But God, everything is so guarded and you can't—there is no way to be orderly about this stuff. But I think part of the fallout from psychedelics and all that has been the gradual sort of disintegration of the old version of the scientific method. You know? The scientific methodology where you plant a whole bunch of the same plant and put a dome over it and slowly poison it. And then say, "Well, this is what happens to a forest," do you know what I mean? That kind of thinking. The kind of, "Do an experiment thousands of times." These ideas are starting to lose some of their juice. And I think that part of that has to do with psychedelics, the experiences that some of the farther-out people in the world and society have had these experiences and been able to project them into what they do.

>>> <<<

JEREMY: Well, I think the last thing I want to ask you about is—this is sort of an odd question, but it's a very central one, it's the question of why are you doing this interview? Which is not by any means to suggest that I'm not grateful, but in a sense that I know you wouldn't be doing this if you didn't have a feeling there was something you wanted to communicate.

JERRY: Well, because I want to be able to say to people in this time . . . where everybody is so roundly against drugs, that, hey, not all drug experiences are negative, you know? I mean, I would like for that minority voice to be heard, you know, that some drug experiences are quite, quite positive and, I think, can be life-enhancing and can be pleasant, and can be not dangerous and—you know what I mean?—don't necessarily promote criminal activity. I think that too much of this thing is the fear of change of consciousness. It's something that I think is something to be feared. It's another level of, you know what, somebody wants us all to see reality the same way or what? You know? I never did get the reason. Now, explain to me again. I understand why it's not good to steal. And killing, I get that. What's the part about getting high again? What was wrong with that? You know what I mean? I don't get the moral, you know, the structural, moral part of it. What is the reason? Why is it that everybody has this thing about getting high?

JEREMY: Well, one of the quotes of yours that I have underlined somewhere is you realized that there was more than what we were allowed to believe.

JERRY: Yeah.

JEREMY: And I wonder who allows this?

JERRY: That's what I wonder. Who is the guy that said—where does it say, even, in the Ten Commandments, "Thou shall not get high. Thou shall not change your consciousness." Who says, you know? The way I understood it is that it was helpful to change your consciousness, sometimes, you know? That's the way I got it, anyway. I just want to be part of that minority point of view. If it is, in fact, a minority point of view.

>>> <<<

It was experiences like the following day at Olompali in 1966 that led to his final point of view.

JERRY: The "all" experience, yeah, that whole day. That included the experience of dying many deaths. It's starting to get more and more kind of a feedback loop of this thing where I was suddenly in the last frames of my life, and then it was like, you know, here's that moment where I die. I run up the stairs and there's this demon with a spear who gets me right between the eyes, you know? Or I run up the stairs and there is this woman with a knife who stabs me in the back. I run up the stairs and there's a business partner that shoots me, boom, you know? And it was like—it's like playing the last frame of a movie over and over, with subtle variations, and that branched out into millions of deaths and all sorts of just visions . . .

>>> <<<

JERRY: I've had some wonderful . . . I mean, for me, some of the scary ones were the most memorable. I had one where I thought I died, like, multiple [deaths]—it got into this thing of the last scene. The last scene of hundreds of lives and thousands of incarnations and insect deaths and then, you know, like, kinds of life where I remember spending some long amount of, like, eons as kind of sentient fields of wheat, you know, that kind of stuff. Incredible things, in these sort of long pastoral kind of extraterrestrial kind of cultures, you know. Kind of bringing-in-the-sheaves sort of thing.

JEREMY: So it went through the dark area and up again.

JERRY: Yeah, right. One time it was really memorable and it actually scared me, but it was also wonderful. And that was one time when I had taken LSD and also, I think, artificial mescaline, possibly. And the LSD was White Lightning, which was incredibly strong and very, very pure. And I remember I was lying on the grass. And we were living, at the time, in kind of a large sort of ranch kind of place in Northern California [Olompali]. The band was all tripping that day. All of us and a lot of friends. And I was lying on the grass. I closed my eyes and I had this sensation of seeing, perceiving with my eyes closed. It was as though they were open, you know? I still had this field of vision. And this field of vision had kind of a pattern in it. It was partly visible, and then I had this thing that the outside of the field of vision was like, started to unravel, like an old-time coffee can, you know that little thing that you spin around, it takes the little strip of metal off. It was like that, and it began stripping around the outside of the field of vision until I had a 360-degree view. And it revealed this pattern. And the pattern said, "All," in incredible neon, you know? [*laughs*] It was one of those kinds of experiences.

5

"The Farthest-Out Person Ever"

Unhappy Egg/Early Work.
Pen and ink on paper.

In *On the Road*, Jack Kerouac described his friend Neal Cassady ("Dean Moriarity") as a "western kinsman of the sun," a modern cowboy version of Prometheus, who brought fire, a fragment of the sun, to mankind, but was doomed to suffer forever for this act. More than a few people thought Neal demented; certainly he brought not a little pain on himself, his friends, his wife, and his family with his compulsive philandering and frequent irresponsibility. A reliable husband and father he was not. At the same time, his remarkable personality and levels of perception inspired not only Kerouac and Garcia but also many others. As Garcia says in different language below, Cassady was the most remarkable man he would ever meet.

Born on the road in Salt Lake City in 1926, Neal Cassady was mostly raised by his father, a profoundly alcoholic barber, on Denver's skid row. By the time he was ten, he was splitting time between the streets and reform school, generally for auto theft, at which he excelled. A local high school teacher, Justin Brierly, was impressed by Neal's evident intelligence and connected him to another of his protégés, a Columbia student named Hal Chase. Visiting Hal with his sixteen-year-old wife, Lu Anne Henderson, Neal first met Jack Kerouac and Allen Ginsberg in New York in 1947, and over the next ten years raced from Lu Anne to his second wife (and mother of their three children), Carolyn, a third (and bigamously married) wife, Diane Hansen, a complex and frequently sexual relationship with Allen Ginsberg, and the transcontinental travels with Jack Kerouac ("Sal Paradise") described in *On the Road*, which, brilliant as it is, only begins to outline the depths of who he'd become.

His obscenely severe imprisonment in San Quentin from 1958 to 1960 cut him off from the tether of his marriage and children; somehow purified by his torment, he emerged as the inspiring, "super heavy" figure Garcia talks about here, a man who'd developed an art form in which *he* was the art, a "Western model

Heidi.
Pen and ink on paper.

for getting high" (as a Zen master is the Eastern model). He fell in with Ken Kesey in the early '60s, drove the bus "Furthur" to New York and other points, and deeply influenced the young men of the Grateful Dead. It was no accident that Jerry's partner Bob Weir would write one of his greatest songs about Neal, his occasional roommate at the Dead's home at 710 Ashbury Street—"Cowboy Neal at the wheel / of the bus to never-ever land"—and finish it, not-so-coincidentally, just as Neal died, on February 4, 1968.

Here, during the session with Al Aronowitz and Jerry's woman friend, Jerry begins by talking about what being around Neal was like.

 Start of Interview

JERRY: Ah, a student in a Zen monastery and having chance encounters with your master, you know? It always blows your mind, and it's always just super heavy. My whole relationship with him was on—I mean, I couldn't describe it. He liked musicians, that was the trip. Neal really liked musicians. He got off on music. He liked my music. He liked my playing. And he loved to dance and he loved to do that crazy shit to the music. And the Grateful Dead was, like, his cup of tea for that kind of stuff. So, you know, me and Neal Cassady and Paul Foster, and maybe one or two others at various different times where you take acid and you get high and you go in a certain kind of place. And it seemed like me and Neal and Paul Foster ended up in this place a lot together. You know? It's kind of like being shipwrecked.

AL: Yeah.
JERRY: You know what I mean?

AL: Right.
JERRY: You can't really—you can't pinpoint what it is that's happening exactly or why, but you know that it's far out and you know that you're thrown together on some far-out level with these other people. And, you know, that was where it was.

129

AL: You found them compatible, where you're working it out.

JERRY: Right. Right. It's tough to talk about.

DENNIS: It is. That's the thing, when I was starting to think, well, it was going—and get all very officious and say, please describe, I'm trying to think of—

JERRY: He was—

DENNIS: —the first time I tripped—

JERRY: —the most far-out person ever.

FRIEND: He was incredibly beautiful.

JERRY: Neal Cassady was.

Neal Cassady, 1966.

FRIEND: He was—looked like a movie star, man. He really did.

JERRY: Yeah.

FRIEND: In pictures that I've seen, incredibly handsome.

JERRY: He looked great.

FRIEND: Yeah.

DENNIS: You described him in that book as a teacher.

FRIEND: A far-out character, *whoo*.

JERRY: Yeah. I mean, that's who he was to me, you know?

DENNIS: Now I'm going to ask an impossible question: what did he teach?

JERRY: He taught me something about doing it a hundred percent. You know? Neal had a real, true, in-control discipline, that governed him, himself, that he used.

DENNIS: Yeah.

JERRY: And he was aware of it, the same as you're aware of—well, the same as he was aware of his ability to drive. He was aware of his ability to keep up and to stay in the present and to, you know, be working out all of the karmic stuff and all these trips simultaneously, and he was aware of when he was on it and when he wasn't on it, you know? And as far as I'm concerned, that's, like, the highest kind of refinement that you can attain. You know what I mean? As far as I was concerned with Neal, there were lots of levels simultaneously. And people thought, like, "Neal's flipped out. Neal's crazy. And Neal's this, and Neal's that." But, you know, he had it all working. He knew what he was doing. He knew how he was doing it. He knew he was taking care of business while he was doing it.

AL: Like his resiliency. Like his way of making losses and defeats seem like victories.

JERRY: I'm not really sure about that. I'm not really sure, because being with Neal was like playing music. You know what I mean? He would, like, throw out a lick, and, you know, I would dig it. It was like that kind of thing. It was like playing music. And you appreciate someone who was so, you know, in time. It's hard to describe. I mean, it hasn't been described so far. It hasn't been said.

DENNIS: Right.

JERRY: And I think he was a guy who was in control of a form that hasn't been classified. But it's like, you know, a Western model for getting high, I think.

AL: First of all, he must have enchanted you as a storyteller.

JERRY: No.

AL: No?

JERRY: My first— Well, let's see, my first big flashes on him were he's the guy for whom talking movies were made. But also a show, you know, also a visual, and the whole thing was like a total expression. My relationship to him at first was seeing him as somebody who was being on, who was on, you know? And I was his audience, initially. And later on, I never listened to, like,

131

132

Astro Biz.
Mixed media on paper.

stories from him, and he wasn't telling stories when he was in that scene. He was doing something else. He was going into the cultural image bank and snapping, you know, with one little thing that automatically would set up a whole series of images and you would understand what was happening. You know what I mean?

AL: Yeah.

JERRY: It was really sophisticated, you know, and really together. And whether or not it was something he was really doing or whether it was something I just thought he was doing, it doesn't matter. The impact was immense. Neal's the farthest-out person that I ever met.

DENNIS: I don't think there's any doubt about that.

JERRY: He was really fantastic. And funny. You know, funny like the kind of funny that's just uncontrollable hysteria kind of funny. Like perfect funny. Really funny. He used to have this hammer, and he'd throw it around and he would be talking and stuff and he would flip it up behind his back, you know, like a juggler would, and he would reach out and catch it and it would fall. And he would do these takes, you know, and all this stuff was going on in, like, the most brilliant slapstick silent movie, whatever, totally physical thing, you know, and really, really perfect, just exquisite.

133

One time after the Watts Acid Test, everybody was, you know, buzzing and pretty weird. It was a weird night. Everybody OD'd and everything. And we were sitting on Hugh Romney's lawn when he was living in L.A., on his lawn and George [Walker, a member of the Merry Pranksters] was trying to park the bus or something, and Neal was, like, really high. He had taken really a lot of acid, and, you know, nobody would let him drive. He was that high. And he was out there and back in the stream of dawn, you know, directing the bus, the way you do in a garage, a little bit left, and all that stuff. But it was like this amazing slow-motion beautiful pantomime. And the bus is slowing backing up and he's directing and doing all this stuff, and he directs it right into this pole. And knocks it over. And then, you know, George parks the bus and Neal picks the sign up, and he's starting to put it up and, you know, and he's doing all kinds of takes, like the famous drunk on the pole, and the pole is weaving and rolling, and he's doing this thing all around it and not saying anything. And there's like two little old ladies on their way to church Sunday morning, walking down the street, and here's Neal out there holding up this post. And all of a sudden he does this whole number with—you know, he starts by trying to hide it behind his back. Those moments, you know, they're, like, perfect. And it was like every time there was, like, that kind of perfection happening, what we need here is a movie camera and a tape recorder and get this shit on tape.

⟫⟫⟫ ⟪⟪⟪

JERRY: Neal was a guy who was like an artist without an art. He was his art, you know? And I watched Neal and I said, if I worked as hard as Neal has in his life to be as much myself as he is himself, I would probably end up the way he is, which is to be just superlative, but really isolated in a strange sort of way. And then at the end of this particular Acid Test, we went and looked at the Watts Towers. And the Watts Towers are interesting because this guy, Simon Rodia, one guy, he went and picked up little pieces of flotsam and jetsam and junk and glued them and cemented them and stuck them together and when he died ... the County of Los Angeles couldn't pull the towers down, so they made them a park. They wanted to destroy them. And I said, if you work really hard as an artist, you may be able to build something they can't tear down, you know, after you're gone. But, hey, what the fuck? What I want to do is I want it here. I want it now, in this lifetime. I want what I enjoy to last as long as I do and not last any longer. You

The Merry Pranksters' "Further" bus at gas station, 1964.

know, I don't want something that ends up being as much a nuisance as it is a work of art, you know? I also don't want to be isolated. I don't want to be an artist suffering in a garret somewhere, you know what I mean? I want to work with other people, you know? So that was the direction I was going in any way with the band and everything. And I've always preferred that collaborative kind of work. I'd rather be part of something than working on my [own]—I don't enjoy myself that much. You know what I mean? Just in terms of, I'm not so full of myself that I can totally develop ideas completely out of myself and love them.

⟫⟫ ⟪⟪

JERRY: [Neal] was completely communicative, a hundred percent, you know, verbally, physically—

AL: To me he was such a great storyteller, like Kerouac.
JERRY: Mm-hmm.

AL: And Kerouac admitted that he copped his storytelling ability from Neal, because Neal, when he would tell a story, he would play every role in it—each voice he would imitate, he would mimic and imitate the person and actually re-create, like an actor, the different people he was talking about.

> **"I've always preferred that collaborative kind of work. I'd rather be part of something than working on my [own]—I don't enjoy myself that much."**

AL: And when he would re-create the dialogue, man.
JERRY: And he would also be like the narrator, and he'd make asides and all that. And it was all in that great language.

AL: Right.
JERRY: Totally. And then he had these little parts that would rhyme, you know. He had like that prison style rhyming trip really down. I mean, he could do it just

all the time. There are some people who learned aspects of that—everybody learned, like, little pieces, bits and pieces of Neal Cassady. There's a certain group of people that if you put them all together in the same building, you'd have Neal there.

AL: Right.
JERRY: You know?

DENNIS: There would be an incongruity, except it isn't with Neal. But I mean, there's this total energy, total communication, and at the same time, as you say, he has it all under control—
JERRY: He didn't always. I said there were times when he was on and times when he wasn't on. And he was conscious of those times. He wasn't, like, acting out something and not knowing what it was. You know, there was a certain image of him in Kerouac's book . . . I think it's probably because Kerouac was always sort of a straight guy. There's always the reservation that Neal could be crazy. It doesn't fully support it. Eventually, Kerouac makes his break, because he couldn't go out on a limb like that, you know? I mean, he couldn't be Neal Cassady. And I think that he was just misunderstood. I think he was misunderstood by an awful lot of people, you know, because of that thing, of knowing when it's there and knowing when it ain't. Knowing when you're on and knowing when you're not. That's the difference between being conscious and being unconscious. And you know, all those things that Neal did that you always hear about, he was doing with that kind of consciousness of what he was doing. He was conscious of how well he was doing all of it.

DENNIS: The question everybody wants to know for themselves, I guess, is how do you figure that out? How do you know when you're on and when you're not on, and how Neal knew.
JERRY: You know, man. You know.

DENNIS: But how do you get to the point—
JERRY: Well, you have to start by doing something that has an on and off to it. In

Neal's case, driving is like a good way to learn that, because when you're off, you're off, man. You die or you blow it, and it's clear. So there's like a real clear on and off.

Ken Kesey and Neal Cassady onboard the Merry Pranksters' legendary "Further" bus in June 1964 in New York City.

AL: But he was a tightrope walker—
JERRY: Yeah.

AL: —and he knew it. He knew what he was.
JERRY: That's it. Like if you were to take up the tightrope, you would understand, on and off on that level. It's like, whatever. If you're doing something and eventually you're doing it well enough to where there's a flow to it, then you know when the flow is there and you know when it ain't. And it's that same thing. But like, most people do it the way I've done it—the way most conventional artists deal with it at that level is to take up a discipline, one specific thing, scope in on it, concentrate your energy on it, like an alchemist, and work on it and work on it, and that becomes the way of telling whether you're on or not, and then all your energy goes into it.

Neal's way of doing that was to eliminate the tool, you know, even though he probably wasn't conscious of it initially and used to envy that discipline. Eventually he became that whole thing—all of his surfaces, if you imagine human beings as having many surfaces, all of his surfaces were on that edge of on-ness and off-ness, and being conscious of whether you're on or off. That whole thing of balancing on the end of a stepladder, you know, the kind of stuff that Neal could do. I mean, when he was on, he could really, because he worked at it, man. He spent a lot of the time doing it. Everybody else thought it was crazy weirdness, but he was working on it.

DENNIS: It's like total concentration.
JERRY: But another kind. An explosion outward rather than the total concentration you have when you're—

137

You know, like playing music is one, would be like—he would consider that one facet, one aspect. Sitting around and bullshitting is another aspect. There's times when it's really flowing and times where there ain't nothing happening.

DENNIS: How did Neal get in touch with Ken? Do you know how he got involved in that whole scene?

JERRY: Just part of the same scene. Probably somebody wanted to score some pot somewhere and somebody knew Neal. That kind of thing, just around.

DENNIS: The question still hasn't been answered and maybe it never will be: How do you think Neal fit in?

JERRY: Nobody fit in.

DENNIS: Well, nobody fit in; everybody was just there.

JERRY: That's why everybody fit in. Well, Neal drove the bus. When he drove the bus, he drove the bus, but above and beyond that, he was Neal Cassady.

138

DENNIS: Yeah, just around.

JERRY: Yeah. And the Prankster scene was open enough and stoned enough to be able to see how far out he really was. I think Kesey is one of the guys that really started to take Neal seriously and really started to understand what he represented in terms of how far you can go with being a human being.

DENNIS: What did Neal talk about, basically?

JERRY: Really anything and everything. I mean, for example, before [an] Acid Test, a lot of times we'd throw a change, the *I Ching*, and Neal would read, you know, like the judgment and stuff. And he would like read a paragraph and say, "See, it's just like I was telling you the other day," and it would all turn into a story, back to the narrative. You know what I mean? It would be multireferential. If he was talking about stuff like cars or something like that, then there would be, like, a certain kind of flow to it. And that was one of the things he would like to talk about, cars and driving. And that was like one of his musical things. But then there was communication on, you know, like that reading the *I Ching*, stuff like that, relating stuff to the now. And he could really go in a lot of different directions and keep it all together. You know what I mean?

DENNIS: Yeah.

JERRY: Not lose you.

DENNIS: Did he ever talk about, let's say, religion in any particular way? You're talking about him as a Zen—

JERRY: Well, no.

DENNIS: —and I can really see that.

JERRY: You have to forget what all those things . . . you have to forget all the Eastern image that goes along with Buddhism and Zen and all that stuff. Just forget all of that stuff and construct in your own mind, you know, i.e., that thing existing in the Western world.

139

FRIEND: You know what he was? He was a successful monk.

JERRY: Yeah.

AL: [*laughing*] Right.

FRIEND: He also was probably a saint because he . . .

AL: Well, he was a saint.

JERRY: Oh, sure, totally a saint.

DENNIS: I know he was into Edgar Cayce [a twentieth-century American psychic, mystic, and healer nicknamed "The Sleeping Prophet" who greatly believed in reincarnation] and that sort of thing.

JERRY: Well, he would mention those things, but those were like notes. It was like the time he said, "It was like Ginsey said," you know. He would relate stuff on the basis of little bits and pieces. You know what I mean? So like, if somebody was talking about something that Edgar Cayce might have once spoke about, he would bring Cayce in, but if somebody else had spoken about it, he would bring that in too.

AL: He read a lot. He read all of Edgar Cayce's books.
JERRY: Yeah, I believe it.

AL: He was really into Edgar Cayce very heavy for a while.
JERRY: I think all that stuff was the stuff that flashed him into far-outness. It was the reason he ended up with the Acid Test, because that represented new horizons, you know, after all the old energy was completely gone. You know?

AL: Yeah.
JERRY: It was new horizons, new bright people, who were into getting real high, you know, and checking it out.

140

AL: Yeah, he was always looking for the new scene and always finding it.
JERRY: Right.

AL: And if not finding it, you know, creating it. Because I mean, after the Kerouac *On the Road* era was over, he had to go someplace else.
JERRY: And there was no place to go for a long time, till LSD came along.

⟫⟫⟫ ⟪⟪⟪

DENNIS: I was just wondering, because it's just—I mean, it seems to me that he made a very conscious attempt not only, you know, to get high himself, but to get other people high too, more and more. I mean, it seems to me that's one of the things he did with Kerouac, was to get—
JERRY: Yeah.

DENNIS: —to work at getting Kerouac high.

JERRY: Right. Well, he could see from some place, you know? From his soul, he could see limitless horizons, and he could see that you could go on forever. You know, I think he was right.

Paul Foster's "Can You Pass the Acid Test?" handbill, colored by Sunshine Kesey, 1965.

Jerry on Playing Music

There is a line, often attributed to the comedian Martin Mull, to the effect of "Writing about music is like dancing about architecture." This of course applies equally to talking about music. Which is to say that music touches aspects of the human condition in ways that cannot be limited to words, simultaneously the refuge and prison cell of our intellect.

In addition to the glory of his playing and the generous wisdom of his leadership, Jerry Garcia's highest achievement may very well have been his frequently stunning eloquence when talking about music—both playing it and listening to it. We began this conversation talking about his role models—not so much other musicians, but other cultural inspirations, like Jack Kerouac. As a historian, I had a fairly clear sense of his connection as an improvisational musician to what Ginsberg called Kerouac's "spontaneous bop prosody," but when Jerry introduced the visual image of the unbroken typewriter roll—a very fast typist, Kerouac had taped sheets of paper together to make a continuous roll that eliminated the need to stop to change paper—I saw it all with fresh eyes. The way Golden Gate Park's design represented episodes fading one from another was a second visual model. And then he started talking about his mental processes and how he approached improvisational playing, and his words became a dance, his playing an architecture. Truly extraordinary stuff.

Warped Guitar.
Colored pen on paper.

Start of Interview

DENNIS: [Kerouac and the Grateful Dead are] two classic examples, spontaneous artists who are sort of the romantic inspirational side of the romantic verses classic equation.

JERRY: Oh, yeah. Absolutely.

DENNIS: And since the critics are always classical and want three-minute form and structure—

JERRY: Right.

DENNIS: —you're gonna get dumped on. And you guys [Kerouac and the Grateful Dead] are two examples of the same progression.

JERRY: Yeah, well, I feel real close to Kerouac for that reason. He really means something to me. That thing of the typewriter rolls. You know? That's so much like my way of thinking. You know what I mean?

DENNIS: Yeah. Yeah. Put it out there.

JERRY: Like a record, that's what you want a record to be. You know? No starts and stops, none of that shit. That seamless stuff, you know, that just works. For me, that stuff works. Other people, it doesn't work for; but for me, it works.

DENNIS: Yeah.

JERRY: I have a love for that kind of stuff. I don't know why. I don't know where it comes from.

DENNIS: I hope I can take a decent guess.

JERRY: There's a lot of places that actually comes from. I mean, really, there are models of it all over the place. In some ways it's basic *Ulysses*, you know, and some places, basically the *Odyssey*. And a real important model for me is Golden Gate Park. And *Fantasia*. Something about the episodes, you know? You can go from one kind of reality to another kind of reality. It doesn't matter how you get there.

And the thing about Golden Gate Park is that if you go from one end of it to another, you find yourself in these different worlds. You know, there's places where all of a sudden it's real prehistoric, looking at those giant ferns, and everything is weird, ancient things. And then you walk a little further and all of a sudden you're in this pasture, and there's sheep grazing and there's a little pond . . . You know what I mean? It changes. And you're not aware of how it's changing or where it's changing, but it does change, and it has a beautiful seamless way of doing that, and it's a work, really. It's like a poem. You know? And you go along and you experience these different realties of it and it's—the gardener, that guy, you know?

DENNIS: McLaren.
JERRY: Yes, McLaren. John McLaren. [McLaren, a horticulturist, was superintendent of Golden Gate Park for fifty-six years.]

DENNIS: Yeah.
JERRY: Really an incredible artist, I think.

DENNIS: Oh, yeah.
JERRY: And for me that's a real expression. That says the kind of thing that I would like to be able to say. And it says it beautifully, gracefully, and perfectly.

DENNIS: It is an interesting universe.
JERRY: Oh, yeah. Shit. It really is.

DENNIS: Yeah, that whole notion of just creating an ongoing succession of different environments.
JERRY: Yeah.

DENNIS: It's as you say, seamless, so that you go from one to the other. And it's like that was in some ways the single first sort of favorite flash for me with the Grateful Dead at my first show—that experience of suddenly realizing that you were playing a new song and on reflection had been playing it for at least thirty seconds, but …there was no overt change. You know?

JERRY: Right.

DENNIS: The Madison Square Garden show last fall, you went—

JERRY: Yeah.

DENNIS: —where you went out of "I Need a Miracle" and you were playing "Bertha" and there was no overt break.

JERRY: Right.

DENNIS: One flowed from the other.

JERRY: Right. I love it when that happens. I love it when it's possible to do that. That's something that I'm better at than I am at other things. That's one of the things I'm good at. Eventually—like, if I have a place to go, eventually, I can get there and make it pretty seamless. Because for me, the relationship between one thing and the other is always obvious. You know what I mean? Even if it's completely invisible to everybody else, to me, it's always really obvious, and all I need to do is know both halves and eventually I'll find the place that works. The walk between the two. Like Weir sometimes does it, but he has sort of a blockier notion, you know? Which is okay; but for me, I like that invisible thing. I like that sort of sleight-of-hand approach. You know?

But I'm learning to be able to appreciate the thing of just clumsily blundering into it, too—it's another color, you know? It's another way of doing that. Like the Grateful Dead for me has been a tremendous mind-expanding experience, because it has ways of doing the things that I like to do that aren't the way I like to do them. You know? But it's taught me all these other possibilities. You know? A lot of which I don't agree with emotionally, but I've learned to appreciate them and learned that they are other kinds of tools. You know? Because, really, when you get

145

down to it, I can be a terrible puritan. It's one of the things that I constantly have to bust in myself, you know . . . I have a desire for too much structure, too much purity, or something. I err on that side of things. I recognize it as a weakness, really. I don't like that about myself. And it's always bugged me.

So I'm constantly having to turn on myself and, you know, suddenly, "Oh, it's that thing again coming up. Oh, shit." You know? This is my own personal battle with my own personality and it may be of no concern to anybody but myself. But for me it's a real war. And the Grateful Dead is good for me for that reason. It's one of the things about it because it always is able to show me something fresh about things like that. You know? Because, musically, I always have an opinion. It's something I can't even avoid, really, but my opinion isn't always the best one. It's just that I always have one.

DENNIS: There are times, you know, when I'll sit there and say, "Goddamn it, I don't care if Garcia and Ram Rod didn't like it tonight. It was great tonight, I'm not going to take their . . . " Sometimes I'll go, "Well, they know better," and sometimes I'll go, "Fuck 'em."

JERRY: No, it's not true at all. I don't know at all. See, that's one of the things that I've learned—I am not the one to judge, by any means. You know? I'm bad at that, in fact.

DENNIS: There are also different ways . . .
JERRY: Different criteria.

DENNIS: Exactly, different criteria. Although, let me ask you something. This is a dumb question, but it's not. When you're playing, do you have, like, conscious thoughts of, "Now I gotta hit this note" or—
JERRY: No.

DENNIS: That you're looking at a place about two feet in front of your nose. Occasionally, you look at other band members, but otherwise, you're pretty much disconnected and you're sort of focusing on feeling your fingers, maybe even looking at them.

JERRY: Yeah.

DENNIS: But there is no conscious thought.

JERRY: No. And I'm not a planner, you know what I mean? I can't do that. For me, reality exists note to note. It isn't extended a little way out in front. You know what I mean?

> "For me, music is like a thing of hunks, you know, of, like, sentences. For me, an idea is not one note. "

DENNIS: At all?

JERRY: Not really. Sometimes there's a big idea out there, you know? Because we may have discussed it—"Well, we're going to do this tune and that tune, that tune and that tune"—but as far as the particulars, and as far as the reality of things, of notes being actually played, I find myself unable to do that even if I strive for it. You know what I mean?

DENNIS: See, that boggles me, because for me, the thing that is most striking about your playing is the inherent sense of structure and of symmetry, so that unlike some guys who feel like it just sounds like, you know, [you're] just basically bashing away for six minutes and then [you'll] come back. It's like, most of the time I can visualize it and—

JERRY: Well, let me put it this way: there is a little more to it than that. I mean, the reality, the existential reality—the real reality is note to note. But the fact is, that for me, music is like a thing of hunks, you know, of, like, sentences. For me, an idea is not one note. You know? An idea is like a sentence or a paragraph sometimes. You know what I mean?

But the nature of it is rubbery. In other words, I don't start out just saying, "I'm going to make this statement X." What it is is more like, "I'm going to start out—I'm doing this thing and it has a certain kind of curvature and a certain kind of thing to it, and it's going to last like four bars," say. I tend to think in even numbers of bars, generally speaking. I tend to think in twos, fours, sixes, like that. So there will be a sentence, it will be X long, like, four bars. And then there will be, like, the answer to that. It will be, like, four bars long, you know? And then there'll be like a summing-up of it, which will be, like, eight bars. And then there'll be like an argument going in the other direction, [and] it'll be eight bars. You know what I mean? It's kind of like that, but as it's going along, there's also things coming in.

DENNIS: From the other band members?

JERRY: Right. Which sometimes, say, like on bar number three, they sometimes say, "No, no, no . . . so my sentence went that way and now—you know—so what I'm going to do to make it syntactically correct is make it so it goes four bars to include that third bar beginning, and then it's only gonna go two more bars for a three-bar sentence. But it'll still maintain the symmetry that I want it to have because it overlaps, taking into account my four bars plus two to include a three-bar idea coming in this way. You know what I mean?

It's kind of like that. I mean, these things are not so conscious, but they're conversational like that. They tend to be sentences. I mean, it has to do with just melodies. You know? For me, a melody is . . . My mind is constantly spinning off little melodies.

I mean, it's like a thing I can tune into. You know? And it's like if I don't do anything, melodies will just start running through my mind. All I have to do is listen to them, you know? Most of the time I ignore them, because they're mostly cheap. But it's just something that's always there. And for me, melodies have the kind of sense that poetry has. They have meter. And so they're like iambic pentameter or something, you know what I mean? Line A of a melody will go like this, and line B will go like that, and so on. C will be *duh, duh* [*indicating music*]. They tend to grow in those kinds of structures, you know? So a melody will start composing itself while I'm playing, and it will start off simple, like an A melody. So I'll say, "Well, that's working," you know? That's something that has a certain gesture to it that's nice at this moment, you know? And so I'll say, "Okay, here's expression A, A. Okay. A again. Um, now, hear B, and B again and then another A to remember"—to bring us back to that moment, you know? And now C and it's like a new discussion, maybe. It tends to be bits and pieces of that—they're syntax, really. They're hunks of stuff like that, like language.

DENNIS: At the root of your whole approach it's like it's always interactive.

JERRY: Oh, yeah. Well, it doesn't have to be. I mean, if I'm sitting around by myself it isn't interactive, it's linear, more linear. But the nature of playing with other people makes it interactive, which also makes it fun. It's part of what makes it fun. And that's just the way it comes out of me. I don't really have that much control over it, you know? So that's where the logic that you perceive comes from, but it's really kind of an illusion. It's not me being logical on purpose by any means.

DENNIS: No, no, but within the fact that you guys play, by and large, the certain fundamental root in R&B blues structure bar, western music to the extent of having sixteen bars and all that.

JERRY: That's right.

DENNIS: There should be some inherent logic arising out of that.

JERRY: That's right. And that's where it's coming from. It's coming from those various roots. That's where the big logic tends to be coming from, you know? And then sometimes I do—because when I'm feeling slick, when we've been playing a lot and everything is working right, you know, my subconscious is working with my fingers. Then I like to do things, like coming in a real peculiar place in the meter and start[ing] an idea there that overlaps it in a completely irregular way. You know? And then start a real big sentence. That's something I do which is less noticeable but it's also structural. The thing is that the structure tends to be much bigger, so it sounds much more like rambling, you know, probably, to other ears.

DENNIS: That's the classic criticism.

JERRY: It's one of those things that's, like I say, the way music works for me. I never decided on it or anything, you know? [That's] just the way it fell in.

149

Penscape/Early Work.
Ballpoint pen and ink on paper.

6

Life with the Dead

Sketches of the band.
Pen and ink on paper.

The conversations here all touch on the early days of the Dead, although topically they skip around. One thread covers the idea of what happens when psychedelic drugs meet improvisational music. In the case of the Grateful Dead, they will tell you, the result was a group mind that became something more than the individuals on stage. It became a thing in itself, something they at times called a dragon. Phil Lesh told me about a science fiction novel called *More Than Human* that describes six flawed humans able to interact telepathically to form a mighty gestalt—a more than fair metaphor for the Grateful Dead, Garcia agreed.

For a band whose stage show involved unspectacular lights, almost no pyrotechnics, and no dance moves—in other words, no significant visual component— the Dead (or rather, their artist friends) would develop an extraordinary library of graphic representations. Given that their name connected to deep folkloric associations, it's perhaps not surprising that artists long before the 1960s had depicted the conjoined concepts of life and death. This connection is illustrated most elegantly by a man named Edmund Sullivan in a 1913 edition of *The Rubaiyat of Omar Khayyam*. Just as synchronicity—or something—guided Jerry Garcia's finger to find "Grateful Dead" in the dictionary, something or other led Alton Kelley and Stanley "Mouse" Miller to the right bookshelf at the San Francisco Public Library early in the fall of 1966.

For a band that had hardly any Hollywood appeal, they certainly had some intriguing adventures with the world of film, most significantly in Richard Lester's *Petulia*. As a film lover and sometime moviemaker, Garcia had fascinating things to say about the experience, as well as his work on the soundtrack of Michelangelo Antonioni's *Zabriskie Point*.

Put any veterans of a rock 'n' roll tour together, and sooner or later they'll start telling road stories. The hard part of rock 'n' roll touring is not the playing, it's the getting there—and who you find in terms of promoters, cops, and hotelkeepers once you've arrived in the next town. Here, Jerry describes the band's first really big gig, one of the most important in the history of rock 'n' roll, the Monterey International Pop Festival, more commonly called Monterey Pop, when the Los Angeles music business discovered that to pull off an authentically hip festival in June 1967, they needed the psychedelic bands from London (The Who, Jimi Hendrix) and San Francisco (Jefferson Airplane, Big Brother and the Holding Company, and the Grateful Dead). It was of course the Dead's enormous misfortune to find itself sandwiched between The Who's spectacular trash-the-stage set-closing routine and Jimi's

Jerry, 1966.

sacrificial guitar-burning ritual. No one, it seemed, was destined to remember their excellent but much less theatrical performance.

Later that summer, they traveled to Toronto and then Montreal in the company of Jefferson Airplane and the Airplane's manager, promoter Bill Graham. This tour was the beginning of a series of hilarious and dramatic escapades, including playing on the roof of the Chelsea Hotel in New York City. By contrast, as a dance band, the Dead encountered enormous resistance in middle America, where folks got very nervous indeed over the idea of young people jumping around and having fun. It wasn't easy being early hippies driving through the Midwest.

The Chelsea Hotel gig had been set up by their friend Emmett Grogan, a leader of the political/theatrical shock troupe the Diggers, who introduced them to the idea of playing free in the park (first at the Panhandle, and later at Golden Gate Park). Jerry then spoke about one of their most unusual gigs, at a gay bar in San Francisco called the Rendezvous Inn.

Martian Base.
Colored pen and ink on paper.

Start of Interview

DENNIS: Phil turned me on to a book that he called the model of the Grateful Dead.
JERRY: Oh, far out.

DENNIS: Goddamn it. I just went blank on the name [*More Than Human*, by Theodore Sturgeon].
JERRY: That's okay. It will come back.

DENNIS: It'll come back. It was science fiction, early forties, fifties, and it's about these four, five kids. One of them is a Mongoloid baby. You know, different kids. All of them are obviously flawed in some fashion, but they get into a—
JERRY: Gestalt.

DENNIS: —telepathic rapport, a total gestalt. And the Mongoloid baby—
JERRY: Is it *The Demolished Man*?

DENNIS: No, no. And when they assume that gestalt, they're, like, superhuman, right. That baby, although it can't communicate except telepathically, is a genius and he calls it the act of blending like that, that it combines blending and meshing, and comes up with bleshing. Now, for Phil, that's the model of the Grateful Dead. Six guys, each of whom has [his] own limits as an individual. That, you know, when it's right and when it happens, can result in this total bleshing onstage, when playing, that is a gestalt that's much higher than what each individual could do.
JERRY: That's a good model.

DENNIS: Yeah, I really like it. Sturgeon, Theodore Sturgeon.
JERRY: Theodore Sturgeon, that's right.

DENNIS: That's the author, anyway . . .
JERRY: I think I remember the book. I can't remember the title, but I remember the book.

DENNIS: It will pop up. I said [to Phil], "When did you first get that sense of bleshing, you know, when you played with the Grateful Dead, the Warlocks?" or whatever. And he said he thought that it had, for him, started happening at the In Room. After a couple of months, but particularly when you go into a situation when you're playing every night for, like, six weeks and you start bleshing.

JERRY: Absolutely. That's about when it started happening for me, too, yeah. And that was what was interesting about it, too. I knew what that meant with bluegrass music, because bluegrass music was formal, and there was the way you did that and the way it worked and it had a whole thing to it, but Grateful Dead music, the Grateful Dead and all that, was not formal and was not traditional. And when it got to that place and did that thing, it was something incredible, you know? It really took off. All of a sudden you had that feeling of, whoa, you know, there is something that's hauling ass here.

⟫⟩⟩ ⟨⟨⟨

Next up, the visual iconography of the Grateful Dead begins for real in late 1966.

DENNIS: Do you remember seeing the original skull and roses that is the Avalon poster that Kelley and Mouse did?

JERRY: Sure.

DENNIS: Do you remember your take on that?

JERRY: I thought it was just brilliant. That is just fab, because as a visual, it so perfectly encompassed the Grateful Dead words. It's like a perfect—

DENNIS: It is.

JERRY: —visual metaphor for the Grateful Dead because of the cheerful roses and the wreath and the sort of happy demeanor of the skeleton guy. It was perfect. I mean, I didn't realize at the time they copped it from *The Rubaiyat of Omar Khayyam.*

> "All of a sudden you had that feeling of, whoa, you know, there is something that's hauling ass here."

Skull Ray.
Pen on paper.

DENNIS: Uh huh.

JERRY: And I didn't associate the images. If nothing else, it was a recognition of a perfect metaphor. And even if it wasn't an original piece of work, it was still brilliant.

DENNIS: They found it.

JERRY: Yeah, those guys found it.

DENNIS: Literally. It's a wonderful story, as a matter of fact. A month before they had done their first Grateful Dead poster for the Avalon, which was Frankenstein.

JERRY: Yes.

DENNIS: And I might add they misspelled the words Grateful Dead, too.

JERRY: Did they?

DENNIS: The first one is G-r-e-a-t.

JERRY: Really?

DENNIS: Rock [Scully, the Dead's first co-manager with Danny Rifkin] took them aside and said, "Now, listen, guys, enough's enough."

JERRY: That's fabulous.

DENNIS: Yeah, isn't that perfect?

JERRY: Yeah.

DENNIS: So they get another assignment. You guys were coming back in September of '66. Just about the time you moved into 710.

JERRY: Yeah.

DENNIS: A little before. [Alton Kelley] said, "Well, Frankenstein was definitely a member of the Grateful Dead, that was cool, but we have to come up with something new." And, literally, they went to the library, you know, where the tall art books are.

JERRY: Yeah.

DENNIS: And he had the same reaction—he said, "Stanley, is this the Grateful Dead or is this the Grateful Dead?"

JERRY: So perfect.

DENNIS: As a graphic symbol, there has been an infinite variety of takes on it and variations.

JERRY: And they all work wonderfully.

》》》 《《《

By 1967, the Dead and their circle were starting to meet people, which led to a near-miss chance to be in one movie (*The President's Analyst*), a more successful part in another (*Petulia*), a chance for Jerry to work with a great (Michelangelo Antonioni) in *Zabriskie Point*, and, in the interview, conversation about other influential films, including *Blow-Up* and *La Dolce Vita*.

DENNIS: You guys got asked to be in *The President's Analyst*. Do you remember that? James Coburn.

JERRY: No, I don't. Did we?

DENNIS: Yes, you did.

JERRY: I'll be goddamned.

Skull and Roses Avalon Ballroom concert poster, designed by Stanley Mouse and Alton Kelley, 1966.

DENNIS: You told Randy Groenke [a fan and researcher] that in an interview. You don't remember that?

JERRY: No.

DENNIS: It's interesting because you said, "Yeah, we got asked." And then you said something to the effect [of], "Well, we aren't going to do it." Do you remember the movie?

JERRY: Sure.

DENNIS: He runs off—

JERRY: With the hippies.

DENNIS: He runs off with hippies and he's playing a gong behind a rock 'n' roll band—you guys would have been the band.

JERRY: Oh, I didn't know that. Oh, yeah, I guess Florence was running around with James Coburn or something like that for a while. She had some contact with him. Yeah, I think if we got an offer, we got it through her. [Rosie McGee, born Florence Nathan, was Phil Lesh's longtime lover and an early member of the Dead's inner circle. She recently remarked on the idea of her "running around" with James Coburn: "HA . . . In my dreams, perhaps. I did meet him and talk to him during that period, but 'running around' with him? Not hardly. I spent some time hanging out at The Castle when we were living in L.A. (in the spring of 1966), the stunning house rented by Tom and Lisa Law, where Barry McGuire and Severn Darden both lived, and Bob Dylan and others spent time. It was through that connection that I met Coburn."]

DENNIS: Uh huh. Well, at any rate, your comment in the interview was to the effect that, "We'll do it, but only if we can control the parts that we're in," and obviously the filmmakers took a look and said, "Right, we can hire nobodies."

JERRY: "Fuck you." Right.

DENNIS: You know?

JERRY: Yeah, right. We always were troublesome to them. There was some other movie.

DENNIS: *Petulia?*

JERRY: Yeah. That was fun.

DENNIS: Tell me about *Petulia*. [The main plot line of *Petulia* concerns the romance between *Petulia*, played by Julie Christie, with a doctor going through a divorce, played by George C. Scott, set against the backdrop of San Francisco just as the hippie subculture becomes highly visible.]

JERRY: Well, there isn't much to tell, really. It only represented about three days of shooting—I mean, as far as we were concerned. One day was location, which is that scene after [Petulia] gets beaten up and she's on her way to the ambulance.

DENNIS: Right, they're carrying her down to the ambulance and you're standing there in your bowler hat going, "Oh, gee, too bad."

JERRY: That's right. We spent the day doing that. And then the thing where [George C. Scott's character] is looking for her in some kind of nightmare disco sort of place, which we're playing in, and that was, like, two days of shooting, I believe. [Director] Richard Lester was a funny guy. He was pretty good—he played the organ a little. Yeah, he sat in and jammed with us a little.

DENNIS: Oh, yeah?

JERRY: Yeah. He was a pretty nice guy. And what struck me about that [was that] for me it was a tremendous learning experience, as far as the art of moviemaking. Because it was a Hollywood production, so they had the vans there and the commissary and millions of union guys and grips and every other fuckin' thing, but Richard Lester basically worked with him, his script girl, his cameraman, and his recordist, and they were the ones that made the movie. Richard would either hold the camera or walk along with the cinematographer. And he would tell him how to shoot. All the sound is wild. He shoots silent like an ad, you know? He doesn't record production sound.

So those scenes when you see me and Weir saying stuff with our little lines, you know, whatever, he recorded those wild. They're not even lip-synched. They're not ADR [automated dialogue replacement], they're not dialogue replacement, they're not dubs. He just got everybody who had lines, who

159

said anything, he put us all on a porch and his recordist was there with his Nagra, and his little mic, and he would have each of us say lines. So, you know, I'd say, "Write if you get work," or something like that, and he recorded them.

DENNIS: Right.
JERRY: And they swap synched them—

DENNIS: Okay.
JERRY: —in the movie. It was fascinating to watch him work because that's the way he worked, with his location stuff anyway. I mean, in the studio, it might have been more controlled and he might have pulled production sound. I have a feeling he probably didn't, though. The sound is too clear, you know, the dialogue is—

DENNIS: Mm-hmm.
JERRY: So I have a feeling he probably made the actors replace all the principal lines.

160

DENNIS: Mmm.
JERRY: Yes, also The Committee [a brilliant improvisational comedic troupe very much part of the San Francisco scene in the sixties that included Howard Hesseman, among many others] worked in that movie, too. So it was fun. Those guys were hanging around all of the shoots too, Garry Goodrow and all those guys, the old Committee and, you know, Janis and Big Brother.

DENNIS: Right, were in that too.
JERRY: So it was kind of a local event . . . I mean, we didn't know what the movie was about or anything, but it was a chance to fuck around. And it was loose enough.

DENNIS: I was thinking of how important [it was that] *Help*—pardon me, *Hard Day's Night*— turned almost everybody's mind around totally about rock 'n' roll.
JERRY: You're right. I got turned on to the Beatles by that.

DENNIS: The new rock 'n' roll.

JERRY: I'm one of the people that got turned on by the movie, not by the records.

DENNIS: Exactly, exactly. And Phil, too.

⟫⟫⟫ ⟪⟪⟪

DENNIS: *Help*, the movie, is the perfect representation of what was called Swinging London, that flowering—David Bailey, *Blow-Up*, Shrimpton, rock 'n' roll aristocracy, that's the perfect representation of that.

JERRY: That and *Blow-Up*.

DENNIS: Yeah, that, together with *Blow-Up*, had the reality—

JERRY: *Blow-Up* is the other big stylistic influence of the sixties. I mean, like Herbie Greene became a photographer after he saw it. I mean, stuff like that. It really influenced people's lives.

DENNIS: It was the greatest. In some ways, it was the most important movie I ever saw in terms of—

JERRY: Style.

DENNIS: At that age—I saw it [when] I was, like, nineteen or something.

JERRY: Yeah, that's it.

DENNIS: And I was just like, oh, wow, there's a whole 'nother reality out there. I think I sat up for twelve hours that night afterward just thinking. It was like total stimulus.

JERRY: Yeah. Right. Us, too. I mean, some of us—you know. There was a handful of movies that were really important movies—I mean, in terms of the effect on our little scene.

DENNIS: Which ones come to mind?

JERRY: *La Dolce Vita* is one of them.

DENNIS: Yeah.

JERRY: Yeah, sure. That one got a lot of discussion. That got endless discussion. I mean, Fellini was, you know—not much weird got into that. There was a theater in Palo Alto [where], you know, because of Stanford and all that, you could go and see Fellini movies or *Blow-Up*, you know, which didn't enjoy general release really when it came out.

"There was a handful of movies that were really important movies—I mean, in terms of the effect on our little scene."

DENNIS: I saw it in a college.

JERRY: It was Antonioni. You know?

DENNIS: When you did *Zabriskie Point* [a highly nonlinear exploration of the counterculture in America in 1970 by Michelangelo Antonioni], did you talk with him?

JERRY: Oh, I worked with him. It was one-on-one. It was a pleasure to work with him, too, because you know, Antonioni.

DENNIS: Right?

JERRY: And I had seen *Eclipse* and I studied his work in a sense. I always was fascinated by his movies. They're so strange.

DENNIS: True.

JERRY: And he is such a stylist, you know? I mean, each movie has a definite look. And he's got that thing of seeing immediately what things are going to be trends. He knows what kind of people, what they look like. You know what I mean? His casting of David Hemmings in *Blow-Up*—

DENNIS: He went looking for that Mark—what's his name? [Mark Frechette.] From the Lyman family? [Mel Lyman was the leader of the Fort Hill Community in Boston, labeled at different times a family or a cult.]

JERRY: Yeah.

DENNIS: Who was the hero of—
JERRY: Right, *Zabriskie Point*.

DENNIS: *Zabriskie Point.*
JERRY: Right, the Lyman family, I forgot about that.

DENNIS: [Antonioni was] looking for somebody with rage.
JERRY: Yeah.

DENNIS: And he found Mark, you know, screaming at somebody on a street. He was, like, bugging somebody or bugging back or whatever.
JERRY: That's Antonioni. When he worked with me he spoke in terms of the music totally in emotional terms. Nothing else. He'd say, "Okay, I want it to be sad here. I want it to be sort of bright and cheerful here. Now, there is something ominous happening." You know? It was all in terms of mood and in terms of emotion, and he was very direct. He speaks English pretty well. He's got a strange stammer. I loved him just right away, you know, but it was one of those maddening situations where just as I felt I was getting started and getting a handle on it, it was over, you know? He said, "No, that's perfect, exactly what I want." I stood there tuning up, "Hey, man, you know? Can't I work on it for a little longer? I'm sure I could get it better." It was one those kind of things. [He was] satisfied way before me.

⟫⟫⟫ ⟪⟪⟪

Our conversation progressed to the band's history in 1967, moving from Monterey Pop to the travails of early days on the road, shows in Montreal with Bill Graham and the Airplane later that summer, a visit to Millbrook, an odd performance on a New York rooftop organized by Digger Emmett Grogan, "The Trip Without a Ticket," and a memorable show at the Rendezvous Inn.

JERRY: . . . [The Who] smashing all their equipment. I mean, they did it so well. It looked so great, you know what I mean? It was like, wow, that is beautiful. You know? We went on. We played our little music. You know? And it seemed so lame to me at the time And [Jimi Hendrix] was also beautiful and incredible and sounded great and looked great. I loved both acts. I sat there gape-jawed. I loved it, man. They were wonderful. You know? And before that, The Who was totally a legend. Nobody knew Jimi Hendrix from anybody.

DENNIS: Right. Right. Opening for the Monkees.
JERRY: Right, I remember Phil's bass got stolen in L.A. the day before we played.

DENNIS: Right. He had to use a backup.
JERRY: Yeah.

DENNIS: And he also got into that weird thing . . . Were you an emcee at Monterey Pop? [Music critic Ralph] Gleason wrote that.
JERRY: Oh. I was on the free stage.

Jerry at Monterey Pop, 1967.

DENNIS: Oh, right. Right. But, no, I mean at the main thing. I want to talk about that, too.

JERRY: Not the main thing? No, no. I introduced somebody over there at the free stage. I don't even remember who it was. It was brief, I'll tell you that.

DENNIS: Brief, but it was also a little more comfortable.

JERRY: Yeah.

DENNIS: Let's see. You did the "Golden Road" and— Wait a minute. [*Dennis reading from a review*]

JERRY: We were always on the trip of free. In fact, we ended up taking all of the Fender amplifiers, and they ended up at the [Potrero] Theatre on [Potrero] Hill. They are probably still there.

DENNIS: Actually, I think Rock shipped them back. Kind of to clean up the karma.

JERRY: Possibly, maybe a few of them. But we got 'em, man. We took those motherfuckers. We ransomed them. I mean, the thing was—like always— they misrepresented to us what it was going to be like. And they didn't put enough attention and energy into the free stage thing, and there were a lot of people outside who were—

M. G.: Couldn't get in.

JERRY: —couldn't get in, yeah. And it was, you know, one of those kind of things. We were always in the middle of those kind of conflicts.

DENNIS: Right.

JERRY: That stuff starts to get . . . I mean, there was a while there when every tour, our second set, you know, the last half of our show, somebody would fuckin' turn off the power, would shut us down.

DENNIS: Yeah.

JERRY: And we started to get fuckin' pathological about it.

Grateful Dead, 1967.

M. G.: You know, it happened all the time.

JERRY: It happened all the fuckin' time. And we started to get crazy behind it. You have no idea what it's like . . . building up and all of a sudden the power is gone. You know?

M. G.: And the audience is there, "wooo"—

JERRY: Someplace in Ohio or some dumbshit college somewhere, and it just makes you crazy. It just made us furious. I mean, goddamn. It seemed like that never stopped happening for one year, maybe '69 or '70 or somewhere in there, right when college campuses were in their greatest upheaval. So everybody associated us, for some reason—I don't know why, God knows we were never very political—but they associated us with danger, you know? As soon as they started seeing people freak out, you know, they thought, "Okay, that's it. We're not going to let this go any further." Boom.

DENNIS: Shut it down. Yeah.

JERRY: Jesus Christ. I mean, that's the evolution, really, of our whole sound system and our power things, you know, with those big fuckin' things that clamp onto the main trunk route—that stuff, I mean, that all evolved from that. We want something that nobody can fucking turn off, ever, you know? It was like they drove us to it, I must say.

DENNIS: "We didn't really mean it that way—we weren't looking for trouble."

JERRY: We were perfectly happy with our regular amplifiers, but they wouldn't let us go on. It was weird. It was so funny. I mean, everybody did it. Bill Graham even did it to us up in Montreal. [*To M. G.*] Remember that time? The audience started freaking out and the cops started getting uncomfortable and Bill Graham told us to stop playing so exciting. "Okay, Bill. Okay. We'll play some lame shit." You know what I mean? What kind of thing is that to say to us? I mean, that's what we're there for. That's what the crowd is there for. That's what everybody is there for, and we knew nobody was going to get hurt. They were all like girls and stuff like that. We knew nobody's going to get fuckin' hurt. It was, like, crazy, but it scared them. It used to be that anything that looked like it was out of control—

M. G.: Well, dancing, freeform dancing—

JERRY: —scared them. Scared the cops—

DENNIS: When you said Montreal, it's like in that free show at Expo.

JERRY: Yeah.

M. G.: People are dancing. That's the one I remember.

JERRY: Right.

M. G.: "People have to stop dancing right now and sit down!"

JERRY: Oh, yeah.

M. G.: Sit down.

JERRY: Stop dancing. I mean, sometimes where they were so hard-assed to the kids. Someplace like Memphis—

M. G.: Or Ohio, University of Ohio.

JERRY: This was a municipal facility because the cops there were regular city cops. I mean, if somebody got out of their chair—if they got out of their fuckin' chair, the cops would come, like three or four big cops, and would come and *bang* them. And I mean, this is during that time when cops were constantly getting onstage, constantly getting in our faces, and we were constantly having to shut [down].

DENNIS: Yeah.

JERRY: It was happening all the time. There would be this six-foot-six cop ready to deck Mickey, you know, or whoever the loudmouth in the band was. And I'd have to jump in there with my guitar and say, "Hey, wait a minute." You know? And the guy would swing at me and I'd have to—fuck, I mean, push them off the stage. It was frequently hairy during those [shows]. I had forgotten all about that shit—

M. G.: Yeah.

JERRY: —until just now. But for about a year, it characterized our shows.

M. G.: I think that gig with the cops was like Toledo, Ohio, or something like that. It was some—

JERRY: There was more than one.

DENNIS: Yeah.

M. G.: I remember it was really scary.

JERRY: I remember one was outside of Kansas City—I guess it was Kansas City— and it was some little soldiers-and-sailors kind of hall. One of those kinds of places. We came out after the show and half a dozen cops were beating the shit out of some skinny little hippie. One of them could have killed him. I remember getting so furious.... The cooler heads in the band had to hold each other back. I mean, it made you want to kill.

It was so cruel and so uncalled for. And it was like, I can't understand this. That was during that period of time when it seemed like our audience was catching shit all the time and our shows were being cut off all the time.

DENNIS: Welcome to the road. You know?

JERRY: Yeah.

DENNIS: You psychedelic guerrillas in the middle of America....

⟫⟫⟫ ⟪⟪⟪

DENNIS: I was going to ask you, as a matter of fact, about that Montreal thing. Well, the funny part of that one is, you did that two weeks in Toronto with Graham—

JERRY: Yeah.

DENNIS: —and the Airplane.

JERRY: They were terrible shows. Oh, we played so badly. There was a huge loud buzz, and we were ready to fire Weir. . . . I mean, the band was in total turmoil during those gigs. We were just coming apart at the seams.

DENNIS: Really? That bad?

JERRY: Well, those gigs were terribly fuckin' depressing. Our stuff didn't work right and the buzz was louder than the music. We were really going completely nuts. We were so relieved to get out of there.

DENNIS: And so you went up to Montreal and you did a free show in the morning downtown on some postage stamp–size stage.

JERRY: Yes.

DENNIS: And then you went out to the Expo.

JERRY: Yeah.

DENNIS: And did it at the Youth Pavilion, I guess.

JERRY: Yes.

DENNIS: And then—

M. G.: With much security. Much, much security.

JERRY: That was the one where Bill asked us to not play so exciting.

DENNIS: Right.

M. G.: Uh huh.

> "Our stuff didn't work right and the buzz was louder than the music. We were really going completely nuts. We were so relieved to get out of there."

171

DENNIS: And then—

JERRY: Then we got off the bus—

M. G.: I remember that well—

DENNIS: And dropped you in downtown Montreal with no gigs to play and Rakow hustled up some rental cars on what's-her-name's money. [Ron Rakow was a former stockbroker and cohort of the Grateful Dead. He was later president of Grateful Dead Records.]

JERRY: Right. Peggy Hitchcock. [Peggy Hitchcock was a member of the extremely wealthy Mellon family that owned Millbrook, the estate that they lent to Timothy Leary as a site for LSD experimentation. She briefly had a relationship with Ron Rakow.]

DENNIS: Peggy Hitchcock. And you went to Millbrook.

JERRY: Millbrook, exactly right.

DENNIS: And then you went down to New York and you played for the Trip Without a Ticket—

JERRY: That's right.

DENNIS: —on the roof.

JERRY: That was really weird.

DENNIS: Tell me about—

JERRY: Shirley Clarke.

DENNIS: Shirley Clarke.

JERRY: What's that famous [play]—*The Connection* [a play by Jack Gelber staged by The Living Theatre. Shirley Clarke directed the film version.]. You ever see that movie or the play?

DENNIS: Yeah, I saw the play.

JERRY: *Connection* is Shirley Clarke. She's the one that wrote that.

DENNIS: Oh.

JERRY: She's got tattoos, cigarette holder. She's like a kind of 1928 Berlin dyke.

DENNIS: Right.

JERRY: You know. And what's-his-face, Andy Warhol, and the Velvet Underground, all that New York—

DENNIS: Weirdness.

JERRY: —you know, that scene. That was the result of Grogan [Emmett Grogan was a friend of the Dead's, a former member of the San Francisco Mime Troupe who had cofounded the Diggers, a political theatrical group that fed the hippies of the Haight. He later wrote *Ringolevio*.] and those guys hustling all those people together. 'Cause they wanted to get bucks.

DENNIS: Right.

JERRY: So we went and played a couple of tunes on the roof at that party and it was at that, whatchamacallit hotel.

DENNIS: Chelsea.

JERRY: The Chelsea. Right. Exactly. Shirley Clarke used to live in the upstairs.

DENNIS: She's definitely a Chelsea—

JERRY: A Chelsea person.

DENNIS: Yeah. Okay. So Grogan got you in there and then—

JERRY: That was weird enough.

DENNIS: Yeah. Very weird.

JERRY: Emmett was a great storyteller. He was another great rapper.

174

The Grateful Dead with Danny Rifkin and Rock Scully on the steps of 710 Ashbury, 1967.

DENNIS: Good Irish—

JERRY: Right. A great bullshitter. He used to come around 710 and tell us about all the scams. "And I was down there with the greengrocers, screaming, and they wanted to give me, you know, twenty pounds of carrots. I said, 'Hey, fuck you. Give me a hundred fifty pounds of carrots.'" And he'd scream at them until they finally just relented. He was that kind of guy. He was able to just scam the most outrageous shit.

DENNIS: Really?

JERRY: Really. He'd always be coming around with big sacks of . . . Remember one time he came around with whale meat?

M. G.: Yeah. God, stinky whale meat or some damn thing—

JERRY: Fuckin' whale meat. I mean, you know, he was just a fabulous hustler. That was like the thing he was best at. He was a very funny guy.

DENNIS: But the Diggers—as far as Danny remembers, and I think it's fairly clear—the Diggers were the guys that got you to play free.

JERRY: Yeah.

DENNIS: And that's a really fundamental aspect of the G. D.—

JERRY: Sure.

DENNIS: Tradition.

JERRY: Right. It wasn't our idea. I mean, we went for it right away, you know? I mean, as soon as somebody mentioned it, "Oh, what a great idea. Sure." You know what I mean? But we never were good at inventing stuff, you know? We were good at going along with it. Yeah. We were agreeable.

DENNIS: [Grogan is] an amazing—the stories of him and—

JERRY: Grogan was good. He was best at self-promotion. He was another guy like Owsley [Stanley, a noted LSD chemist and the Grateful Dead's sound man], you know, one of those highly visible, invisible—

DENNIS: Invisible.

JERRY: —guys.

DENNIS: True. True.

JERRY: He was another one of those guys—you never saw pictures of him anywhere, but you heard his name everywhere.

DENNIS: Right.

JERRY: And everybody knew him. You know? So he was one of those kind of guys, Emmett was. He was a pretty good writer, too, not bad.

DENNIS: As a story, *Ringolevio* is gripping, you know, keeps you going and—

JERRY: I really liked *Final Score* [Grogan's crime novel], yeah.

〉〉〉 〈〈〈

JERRY: I'll tell you, one of the weirdest gigs we ever played was one we played back when we were at 710 Ashbury early on [May 1967]. These guys came over and they were from this place that was a gay bar.

DENNIS: The Rendezvous Inn.

JERRY: You know about that?

DENNIS: Yeah, but go on, go on.

JERRY: It was incredible. And the guy came who owned it. He was like an older, really immaculate looking gentleman, you know? And he had a young boyfriend and they were both . . . they both looked great. We got hired for this gig and we were game. Sure, hey, yeah, twentieth anniversary of a gay bar, what the fuck, you know?

DENNIS: So it was a one-shot.

JERRY: Yeah, it was a one-shot. We went there and played and the audience was all men and this was in the days before guys were out in drag. So nobody was in drag, not a soul, and there were all these handsome young men. You know? It was so strange.

DENNIS: And they went wild over Bobby.

JERRY: A wonderful audience. They were just great. They were just as nice as can be and they all politely kept their hands off Weir as we walked through the crowd. You know what I mean? It was just—they were so well behaved. It was such a nice trip, but the unusual thing, there were no chicks, not a single chick there. That was the thing that was weirdest.

DENNIS: Right.

JERRY: —looking out there and not seeing any girls.

DENNIS: Say what?

JERRY: No girls. I remember being impressed by how really nice they were. They went out of their way to not put us on a weird trip. You know? It was like they were really being nice to us. I mean, I grew up in San Francisco—I was around gay people all my life.

DENNIS: Barney [Laird Grant, aka "Barney," a friend of Jerry's since junior high school and the Dead's earliest crew member] talks about he and Pig—the audience, certainly—

JERRY: Oh, yeah.

DENNIS: —was aware of Bobby and—

JERRY: That was fabulous.

Young Hero, Bobby Weir.
Colored pen on paper.

Playa Vista.
Colored pen on paper.

DENNIS: And the two of them said, you know, they were patting him on the ass
and calling him "Candy."

JERRY: Yeah. Right. They were—but they weren't rude.

DENNIS: No, no.

DENNIS: No. They were just being appreciative.

JERRY: Yeah. They were a good audience, man. They were really polite. I mean, we
played to way worse crowds.

DENNIS: I'll bet, I'll bet. Yeah. The Rendezvous Inn.

JERRY: It was up one flight. Nice place. Not a bad place, not a bad room either.
Even had a little stage and everything. Kinda small even for us, even in
those days . . .

〉〉〉 〈〈〈

JERRY: In those days, the way we used to travel was we would get off the airplane—we usually made our big jumps in the airplane—we would get off the airplane and climb into VW vans that local hippies owned, because in those days the promoters and stuff like that were hippies. I mean, like in Detroit and all those places. Any place that we'd go just about was a pretty funky scene. And we didn't even get rent-a-cars. We would just get picked up and stay at somebody's house. You know? That kind of stuff. And so we were used to that. We were used to it barefoot. You know what I mean? I mean, that was not a problem for us, really.

There was one time I remember we went to Cincinnati or someplace like that. Kesey was there and the Hog Farm. [A hippie family so-named because they had, at one point, lived at a pig farm. They were led by Hugh "Wavy Gravy" Romney and became famous doing "security" at Woodstock.] And we ended up in a dormitory kind of affair, everybody in the band in one room. But we were still used to that shit by then. It was no hardship. You know?

DENNIS: That was '70, as late as 1970.

JERRY: Yeah. We were still doing that shit by '70.

M. G.: We were scuffling hard in 1970, as a matter of fact.

JERRY: By the time Bill opened the Fillmore East, then our fortunes took a turn for the better. Then we started riding in limos—I mean, we were starting to do well. Not our records or anything. But our shows were doing well. And in New York—I mean, once you make a splash in New York, once you've got a New York audience there, it's like you own the town. You know what I mean? In New York we could do any fuckin' thing.

Jerry on Politics and the One-Person Universe

Jerry had little interest in electoral politics or the '60s movement—as Rock Scully once joked, "Our revolution is on the molecular level." But that didn't prevent Garcia, as usual, from making some very perceptive and insightful remarks about how people interacted and why he found the concept of governance so silly. He begins with the literal, the first election to attract his attention, addresses the "us versus them" mentality of '60s movement politics, and concludes with a tour-de-force set of comments on how the world revealed to him by LSD required that all people be addressed as unique individuals. It resembles the Beat scene in its apolitical quiescence, but philosophically, it's what would have happened if you'd fed Henry David Thoreau a fat cap of Purple Haze.

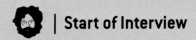 | **Start of Interview**

DENNIS: Do you remember the first election you . . .

JERRY: Yeah. I remember it was in '48. It was the Harry Truman one because of the voting machines as a little kid. They had a little kid-size voting machine in the voting place up around the corner from my aunt's house . . . I don't remember having the slightest interest in it. I just remember it was about Harry Truman and that was the Dewey one, but I don't remember anything about that. I just remember the voting machine. That was the main thing.

DENNIS: Have you ever voted?

JERRY: Yeah, I voted once, and I hated myself for it. I voted for Johnson against Goldwater. I always regretted it. I mean, I regretted it for being put in that dumb place and voting for the lesser of two evils. You know, I get the same problem this election, too [the 1984 presidential election in which sitting Republican president Ronald Reagan ran against Democrat Walter Mondale]. You know, as badly as I would want to vote against Reagan, I can't vote for Mondale. I do not like the guy.

DENNIS: I'm not fond of him, but I feel this absolute obligation to vote against Reagan and the only real, you know, sort of literal way is to vote for Mondale.

JERRY: Yeah, I know, but you know something? I fear Mondale as badly as I fear Reagan. I really—I feel that Mondale has it within him to fuck up things very badly.

DENNIS: The one specific way that I am absolutely convinced he would be better, and that, for me, is the ultimate critical one, is Supreme Court justices. There are going to be at least three vacancies—

JERRY: There's that.

DENNIS: —in the next four years.

JERRY: Yeah, there is that. There is that. I'd hate to be stuck with a Reagan Supreme Court for another twenty years. [*sighs in disgust*]

DENNIS: That's it, man, you know, we lost the Fourth Amendment a couple of months ago. What about all of the rest?

JERRY: Right, it's gone.

DENNIS: And it is terrifying.

JERRY: I agree there is something to that, but I just . . . My conscience won't let me—you know, I just can't. You know, I really can't . . .

⟫⟫ ⟪⟪

DENNIS: You guys have a weird politics, taking politics in a very broad sense.

JERRY: Yeah.

DENNIS: And the politics being again basically anarchist and just basically antiauthoritarian. But in that period, what made a difference, say, then from now was that sense of us and them. You know?

JERRY: Yeah.

DENNIS: There was us, the hip people versus . . . you know, it was a versus situation. Whereas now it's basically us and them, but we ignore it rather than parade it, to some extent. Whereas then, there was a great deal of pride in being us, you know? Now it's just, we're all doing whatever we feel like doing.

JERRY: Right.

DENNIS: But that is a political statement of sorts.

JERRY: Well, for me, acid had opened up some new categories in that level. Somebody else said something funny about that "us and them" stuff. There was a moment in there when it might not have gone that way. Where things were still funny enough and loose enough and nonthreatening enough that it hadn't polarized to us and them-ness, quite. I prayed for that third way. And it might have been possible for another thing to happen, but it didn't, you know? Another thing was, like, looking to happen. It just didn't. It would have been the long shot. It would have been the long-shot possibility that would have eliminated the "us and them" polarity because it didn't need to happen. It didn't really need to happen that way, but that's the way things always fell down, the way they always do. They tend to—because somebody starts getting on that "us and them" thing. And it was really the legality finally that did it.

It was really the cops again, you know, and dope and that context. . . . You know? Which is really, totally inappropriate for the times and everything.

DENNIS: There's always a cop around.

JERRY: Yeah. But it was always hard for me to think in political terms, though. I mean, I didn't think that way then at all, really, and I didn't tend to see things in terms of being political kind of problems with political kinds of solutions. For me, things don't fall down that way. I see the one-person nation, you know what I mean? I see the world that way, realistically, you know? I mean, the whole idea of government is like a ruse. Anybody who thinks they're really governing is silly. If it happens, it only comes from the thing of whoever's got the biggest threat, and that's only scaring people and herding them around. It's not governing, by any means. There's only—there's the one-person nation. You know what I mean? Each person is a nation. There's too much to people. Acid taught me, if anything, that people are limitless. There is more to any one person than you can ever imagine, you know, and you could never—it's not smart to try to put people into lumps; they don't go that way. Each individual person has way too much to them. There's too much detail to them. There is too much individuality there. You can't ignore all that stuff. The individual person can't. The person who is inside it can't. They're stuck with who they are. The only thing that seemed realistic was to respect each person as an individual universe. I mean, that is about large enough. You know?

DENNIS: I hear you.

JERRY: I couldn't see how you could get it any different than that and be anything but bullshitting yourself about it. Even the governments that exist, such as they do, are really just silly structures.

DENNIS: True. True.

JERRY: If they enter your mind or your life or your consciousness at all, they tend to enter as some foreign alien bullshit thing that you have to deal with, you know, in an irritating sort of [way]. That's not the way things should be. Humans are . . . all this evolution makes us better than that. We're not for that bullshit. Stuff is all too small and too chicken shit for humans.

DENNIS: True.

JERRY: For me, psychedelics were that, you know. It gave me a sense of the value of the individual human . . . I can't shake it now. I'm sort of stuck with it now. And it makes it hard for me to think in the kind of easy ways that politics has of looking at things. Just the fiction that people are governable. That's . . . Come on.

New York doesn't run, doesn't exist because it's governable, you know what I mean? It runs because those people are willing to believe, each one of them, that they're going to hold it together for one more day, you know? It's a working chaos, you know what I mean? It's a functioning chaos. It isn't controlled. You can't control a place like New York. Come on.

DENNIS: Totally. Long since out of control.

JERRY: Absolutely. Right. But there it is. And I believe that you can trust that one person per nation, you know what I mean?

DENNIS: Yeah. That's the core.

JERRY: The other way is that you can't trust it, so you have laws and all this other bullshit. I don't believe that. But that way of thinking is so radical that I can't even—

DENNIS: Again, it's that romantic versus classic—

JERRY: Right.

DENNIS: You know?

JERRY: I trust the human.

DENNIS: Exactly. And the classic doesn't, though.

JERRY: Yeah, right.

⟫⟫ ⟪⟪

JERRY: Since people can be whatever they think they are, they might as well think that they're something great, you know? They might as well start high and work down from there rather than start at the bottom and have that to overcome, you know? It's so much harder. Jesus.

DENNIS: Yeah, yeah.

JERRY: And in, you know, Garcia world, one of my best shots at it was this place where when you're three years old, everybody would be issued an unglamorous but extremely lethal weapon that didn't make any noise and didn't flash or anything like that. And when you wanted to do somebody away, you just point it at them and pull the trigger and they would just vanish immediately and then you would vanish shortly afterward. You know? That would be it. So everybody would have one chance to be lethal in their life, but it would cost them their life to do it. That would solve the problem of—

DENNIS: Violence.

JERRY: —who dies. Who lives and dies, violence and all that, you know? So everybody who is violent would take themselves out pretty quick, you know, like that. And then there would also be instant retaliation or whatever. You wouldn't have to wait around for laws and courts and all that, so you dismantle all that stuff. You don't have that to worry about, and it would give everybody absolute equality in a life-and-death way, you know? There would be no more bullshit about who's got power and who doesn't have power. Everybody would have the same absolute life-and-death power, you know? You'd start there, and either everybody would get it together with a kind of manners that it takes to stay out of trouble, you know, and thus survive that. Or else people would have longer tempers, being careful not to kill somebody because they'd know they'd have to go with them, that would make them a little more tolerant. Something along those lines is about the only thing I could come up with that I thought would make it possible for you to dismantle all of the bullshit of civilization, I mean that has to do with governing and controlling people—jails, courts, laws, governments, so on and so on. And everything then proceeds in a basic one-on-one transactional kind of way, without anybody ever being able to get the absolute upper hand of anybody else because there is always that threat. So if he's enough of an asshole, somebody would be willing to sacrifice their lives to get rid of him. That was the only way I could think of that might work.

DENNIS: Yeah. Increasingly the problem in our society now is a lot of people, like that guy down at McDonald's in San Diego [a mass murder in San Ysidro, California, on July 18, 1984], who want to die and don't have the balls to do it themselves.

JERRY: That's right. And that's bullshit, that's chicken shit. And also the gun is too glamorous.

DENNIS: Right. So they go out, they watch too much TV and go out in a blaze of glory just like on *The A-Team*.

JERRY: Yeah, it sucks. That whole violence thing is bad news. You know, it's . . . who needs it? But things are so *wrong*, you know what I mean? The mistakes have been made—were made so long ago—the *wrong* decisions were made, and then the idea of sticking to them, you know, all that stuff got decided so long before we got here that we never got a chance to vote on any of it.

DENNIS: Dig it. Dig it. We're fairly stuck in the swamp and mostly wiggling at this point.

JERRY: That's right. That's one of the reasons it makes it rough for me to vote at this point, you know what I mean? It's like, I don't know how to solve problems at this point, but I don't think I can vote my way out of my moral dilemma of being in this world. Somewhere along the line I have to get a moral grasp on things, you know? And I can't feel it out. I can't find it in trying to do things to what's there. I can't see how I can do things to what's there without making them worse than they already are, you know what I mean? Or at least the potential is there for me to add my energy into making that worse than it is. So maybe I can withdraw from it and maybe if it doesn't have my energy, maybe some part of it will fall off, drop off and die, you know? Maybe not, but—you know. That's the thing. See, I don't know whether that's a viable solution, but so far it's the only thing I've got in lieu of a better way to act. I would like to be able to act. I mean, the way you'd want to be in life is to be able to use all of your positive energy and have it forthcoming all the time. But life doesn't let you do that, really. The world doesn't let you do that, not full time.

7

1969: A Year of Changes

There was just something completely weird about 1969 for the Grateful Dead. They always thought of their performance at Woodstock as a complete disaster—it's difficult to perform when you can hear people behind you yelling, "The stage is collapsing." Recently released footage shows them playing under lighting too faint for filming. The real problem was that they'd tried to jump-start their limited time on stage by opening with a big number, "St. Stephen," but they mostly threw themselves off their game. They rallied, but they largely remembered the pratfall.

Altamont, which was planned to be the West Coast equivalent of Woodstock, this time with the Rolling Stones headlining over the San Francisco bands, became a real disaster when it was moved at the last second from Sears Point Raceway (which had a working setup) to the Altamont location. In a glorious fit of "the show must go on," they tried to put on an enormous show (hundreds of thousands of people in the audience) on a two-foot-high stage, and the Hell's Angels, whom the Dead had vouched for, proved to be unpleasant security guards with a portion of the crowd that was filled up on equally ugly drugs. To top it off, the Dead didn't even get to play.

In that era, they endured a huge amount of grief from early promoters who would supply lousy sound systems and poor security, and police who abused their audience. They made hardly any money, and one night they were victimized by one of the worst psychedelic disasters in their history. During a run at the Fillmore West between June 5 and 8, 1969, a man named Ken Goldfinger put an extraordinary amount of LSD in the apple juice backstage. The consequences were widespread and in some cases severe. Jerry begins by talking about Terry the Tramp, a Hell's Angel friend of theirs, who that night kept an eye on an incapacitated Robert Hunter.

Jerry goes on to talk more generally about how he coped with too much LSD during performances, and then to the central irony of 1969 for the band; in the middle of a sea of troubles, they were making the finest experimental, psychedelic, jazz-rock fusion music by anybody ever. At the same time, they were preparing material that would lead them to the biggest transformation of their musical lives, wherein they'd add a new dimension of brilliant songwriting that referenced the emerging acoustic-folk-country-rock scene. The two albums they recorded the following year, *Workingman's Dead* and *American Beauty*, spoke to the larger public and greatly enlarged their audience and popularity. One of the central elements of this change was Jerry's discovery of a pedal steel guitar and how, due to special circumstances he talks about here, he was able to grasp some essence of it.

189

In keeping with the theme of this very weird year, the chapter ends with a discussion of the 1969 Light Show strike, when the San Francisco rock community turned on itself.

 **| Start of Interview**

JERRY: One night [Terry the Tramp] sat up and babysat with Hunter when Hunter was stoned on acid after the big freakout at the Carousel Ballroom, when somebody overdosed the apple juice—you've heard about that?

DENNIS: Goldfinger.

JERRY: Yeah. That's when Christie had just gotten to the United States after a long absence. Christie Hunter [Christie Bourne, Hunter's lover, although they did not marry].

M. G.: Oh, God. That was awful.

JERRY: She ended up out in the fuckin' graveyards in Colma, stoned on acid, you know?

DENNIS: Rhonda [Hagen, wife of crew member John Hagen] went into convulsions and—

JERRY: Yeah. Right. And Hunter ended up over at Nicki Scully's place with Terry the Tramp sitting up, babysitting him. And I got a call from them in the middle of the night when we were living in Larkspur to go over there—

M. G.: Well, Hunter had a black eye. Somebody—

JERRY: No, no, no. Owsley had a black eye. Hunter punched him.

M. G.: Hunter punched out Owsley!

DENNIS: I thought Janis wasted Owsley—

JERRY: She might have, too. Hunter caught him out of—Hunter was lying on Market Street—

Jerry, c. 1969.

M. G.: It wasn't even Owsley's fault.

JERRY: He said lobsters from the ninth dimension were devouring downtown San Francisco. And all of a sudden there was Owsley's face and he just had to take a swing at him. In fact, when I saw him, the first thing that came out of his mouth was, "Owsleystein. Owsleystein!" He's there mumbling and muttering shit.

M. G.: He was so out of it. I remember you went to get him.

JERRY: Yeah, I went to—

M. G.: The call came about nine in the morning.

JERRY: There is Terry the Tramp sitting with him as nice as can be and just looking after him and "I just want to make sure he doesn't hurt himself."

M. G.: How did we get home?

JERRY: We drove home. I drove us home.

M. G.: We drove home about five miles an hour.

JERRY: Weaving through the hallucinations.

M. G.: Past the Golden Gate Bridge. It was foggy.

DENNIS: Oh, God. Oh, yeah.

JERRY: And then I had to drive back to San Francisco—

M. G.: Yeah.

JERRY: —to get Hunter, you know, and I was barely able to deal with it myself, but Hunter was gone. He was like nineteen sheets to the wind, you know? He was really out there. Poor fucker. He was really stoned and he was just coming into the "bringing in the sheaves" part of his acid trip, you know what I mean? After . . . ah well, you know, the golden light of Buddhism glowing off in the distance somewhere and all that shit. I mean, he was done in. And I sat there, and that was just after that Crosby, Stills, and Nash

Jerry and Owsley "Bear" Stanley, c. 1968.

record first came out, and Nicki was playing that on her home hi-fi, and I got imprinted by listening to that record about nineteen times while I was waiting for Hunter to get to where he could walk around.

DENNIS: That was confusing the hell out of me, and the reason why—

JERRY: It confused all of us, man. Don't feel like the Lone Ranger. Poor Phil. Phil had to be led onstage.

DENNIS: By Mickey.

JERRY: I don't even know if we played that night. Yeah, we played. We were out of it.

Facets 2.
Airbrush on paper.

M. G.: That was bad. That apple juice went around that room and everybody put something in it.

DENNIS: I gather Goldfinger was the chief contributor.
JERRY: Disaster. I mean, I just—I wet my lips on that and that's *all*. I'd heard it had been dosed. I thought, what the fuck?

M. G.: Yeah, me too. I took one tiny little sip.
JERRY: And I got really stoned.

M. G.: Yeah. I remember I took a sip that was probably a teaspoon and a half full. "I'll just try that. I'll just let that bit do." Twenty minutes later, there were people just—

DENNIS: Flopping.

M. G.: —coming apart all around me.
JERRY: There's the truth. What a disaster.

DENNIS: Right. I can tell you now, but it was actually Fillmore West, I think you'd find.
JERRY: I guess it was—either way, it was at the Carousel building.

DENNIS: Exactly. That's what had confused me, though.

M. G.: On the familiar old sofas.
JERRY: Yeah. Yeah.

DENNIS: Yeah, that was—it was about spring of '69.
JERRY: That sounds about right.

DENNIS: Fillmore West. There we go. March—among the great shows.

M. G.: Yeah, March, early spring; that's what I remember.

DENNIS: Well, you played February 27th and March 2nd. March 1st, I might add—
JERRY: That wasn't—Janis's band wasn't playing. Miles Davis, I think, was playing.

DENNIS: Miles was a year later.
JERRY: Who was it that was playing with us at that show?

DENNIS: Junior Walker.
JERRY: Junior Walker & the Allstars.

M. G.: Oh, God.

DENNIS: And Snooky [Flowers, saxophone player in Janis Joplin's Kozmic Blues Band] was in there somewhere.
JERRY: He was just visiting.

DENNIS: I guess visiting.
JERRY: Yeah. Him and Janis just came by to visit. And, of course, poor Snooky got totally wiped out—hasn't been the same since, needless to say.

DENNIS: Yeah, that's right.
JERRY: I mean, he's happy about it—he's a happy hippie. I mean, you know? He never minded that.

> "And I sat there, and that was just after that Crosby, Stills, and Nash record first came out, and Nicki was playing that on her home hi-fi, and I got imprinted by listening to that record about nineteen times while I was waiting for Hunter to get to where he could walk around."

195

DENNIS: Good.

M. G.: That was terrible.

DENNIS: That, from all accounts, was the ultimate—

M. G.: It was an assassination.
JERRY: A disaster. That one and the one they called the Celestial Synapse, the one that Don Hambrecht guy put together where everybody got a card with an STP [Serenity, Tranquility, and Peace—a synthetic hallucinogen] tablet in it.

DENNIS: I wasn't aware of that detail. That was a very elaborate, printed invitation.
JERRY: Yeah, the invitations included an STP tab.

M. G.: Oh, God. Ugh!
JERRY: That was the one where naked people festooned the stage.

DENNIS: That was in February—
JERRY: That was in the big O.D. period.

DENNIS: Spring '69 seems to be fairly—
JERRY: Oh, man, it was incredible. That's partly where we got our reputation for dosing people. Although we never dosed anybody, at least not on purpose.

DENNIS: Yeah.
JERRY: At least not very often.

DENNIS: Yeah, not often. Although, I do know of a large jar of tabs—
JERRY: Yeah –

DENNIS: —sitting on the [stage]—and being thrown. But to me that's not dosing.
JERRY: No.

DENNIS: You put it in your mouth. That's up to you.

JERRY: Right. We were never involved with dosing—that kind of dosing where people didn't know. It was always one of those things where if you want to get high—

DENNIS: Well here, here you are—that's a totally different matter.
JERRY: Yeah.

>>> <<<

JERRY: I couldn't handle it, either, but I mean, I just did what I had to do. I mean, for me it was one of those things where I would have those kinds of fantasies where if I didn't go out and play, I would die. I mean, that's the way my mind worked. I remember one time—

Monster/Mobster Scene.
Mixed media on paper.

DENNIS: Good old Irish guilt.
JERRY: Yeah. We played at the Fillmore, but Bill wasn't running it. It was after Bill.

DENNIS: Right. The Kramers.
JERRY: Yeah. And we played there and somebody brought a cake, you know, and I looked at it and I said, I know that motherfucker is dosed. I just know it's dosed. I said, well, shit, I'll just have a little frosting. You know? The frosting had, like, five hundred hits of STP and two hundred hits of acid. And I was just—gaaah. This night I'm sitting here in this room and this guy comes in and he looks just like me. You know, it's like some guy who was . . . he looked

just like me, you know what I mean? And obviously, he's just waiting to pull this number on me. I don't think he knew I was stoned on acid, you know? I looked at him and it was too weird. It was more than I could deal with. And there were these other weird people, you know, like dealers and things like that, and I got into this fantasy where the mafia was going to kill me—I had this paranoid thing. Well, the only thing to do is to go out onstage and I'll just play for my life.

DENNIS: Actually, that makes total sense.

JERRY: Yeah. Well, it always worked for me. And it always made it so that I would just put all of my anxiety into the music. Not in that sense—but it was like a release. It was like—it was like a prayer. You know? "You let me survive this, I will play so well."

DENNIS: "I promise."

JERRY: "I promise I'll practice every day."

198

DENNIS: "Brush my teeth."

JERRY: Yeah, it was kind of like that, and I mean, ever since then, when I get dosed, which still happens to me. I mean, it still happens occasionally. And I know there is not a fuckin' thing I can do about it. What am I going to do?

〉〉〉 〈〈〈

JERRY: The Acid Test was like the real great training, but that one show where I was able to—I mean, I was way too stoned to function, frankly. I just played for my life. It was that simple. That made it real easy, and it's always worked for me and it's very natural by now.

DENNIS: There was also a time at the Carousel where you didn't. You were too stoned, at least, for a while.

JERRY: Oh, yeah.

DENNIS: And what happened was you suckered Elvin Bishop—

JERRY: Oh, yeah.

DENNIS: —into going up and sitting in—or you, or Phil.

JERRY: Phil was too stoned one time, I remember. He couldn't play. He just couldn't play. It was like he was so out of it. I think that was at . . . maybe it was a radio station benefit.

And Elvin Bishop, right, came up onstage and we just did nine million choruses of the blues, which worked out okay.

DENNIS: "Right, so Elvin comes up and he kicks off a blues song. He's playing sixteen-bar blues. I'm playing"—this is Phil speaking—"I'm playing thirteen bar, Weir is playing a seventeen-bar blues."

JERRY: [*laughing*] Right.

DENNIS: "We tried to do two songs, man. And the look that Elvin Bishop gave me as he walked off the stage, I'll never forget as long as I live. It was complete and total incomprehension."

JERRY: Right. Poor Elvin. You know?

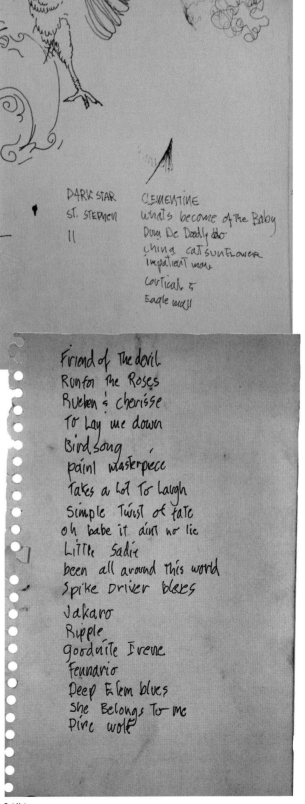

Set lists.

DENNIS: This was the dose night! [More Phil.] "Junior Walker was playing with us."

JERRY: He was not operating that night.

DENNIS: "I was so fuckin' stoned . . . Janis was so mad. Found everybody in the Grateful Dead and put them up against the wall."

JERRY: Right. Janis was ready to kill us. It wasn't our fault, but she was ready to kill us.

DENNIS: This is a great line about that night [Reading again from Phil's interview]: "There was Snooky. There was Janis raving up there just—aaaah—Phil looked up at the light show"—this is Frankie Weir talking—"on the back wall and when I met his eyes, I also looked and we looked at each other and he said, 'Nero burning Rome.' It was really flames. That's what I saw."

JERRY: Nero burning Rome. Phil is incredible.

⟫⟫⟫ ⟪⟪⟪

In fact, 1969 was one of the oddest years in the history of the Grateful Dead. At the same time that they were playing the wildest, most psychedelic, most cosmically far-out jams, they were getting ready to make an enormous pivot in their music, to reach out and do something quite different—not instead of, but in addition to. Along with a sizable selection of the rest of America's rock bands, they were going to come in from the chilly winds of psychedelia and engage the warm, fireplace glow of acoustic folk and country music. There were many sources for this evolution, and being the Grateful Dead, it was natural that at least one major element in the transition was entirely random; after years of curiosity, Jerry encountered a functioning pedal steel guitar in a store and had something of a revelation.

DENNIS: You started out as a—what did somebody call it? A slightly freaked R&B band.

JERRY: Yeah.

DENNIS: With a heavy accent on the blues, and then from that gradually into the experimental band that recorded *Anthem of the Sun* and hired Tom Constanten and got really weird.

JERRY: [*laughing*]

DENNIS: And in April of '69, you bought the pedal steel, started fooling with that, and then as the summer went on with Marmaduke and all kinds of other things. Plus simultaneously, you're living with Hunter in Larkspur and you start working out the acoustic material.

Not for Kids Only.
Mixed media on paper.

JERRY: Yeah.

DENNIS: And eventually—
JERRY: We started doing a lot more singing then, too.

DENNIS: Right, well, that's the thing.
JERRY: Yeah.

DENNIS: And to me, that's the ultimate change. The most single distinctive thing in the history of the Grateful Dead . . .
JERRY: Yeah.

DENNIS: But you made a conscious decision, or at least unconscious decision at some point, that rather than go on and be the ultimate experimental forty-five-minute "Dark Star" band—you were going to try and be complete musicians and sing as well as, you know, jam and write interesting material that people could relate to.
JERRY: Right. Well, that was definitely pulling me. I mean, that was something that was happening to me.

DENNIS: A lot of times in interviews you've mentioned the fact that Crosby, Stills, and—well, Crosby and I guess Stills were around.
JERRY: Yeah, that was definitely something, because they made it seem so easy. Well, it's the most natural thing on earth, you know. And it was fun to do. It was something that we could do . . . And when we found ourselves—when we did it, it sounded so cool. And just sitting around with an acoustic guitar and working up those songs . . . it sounded pretty, and, "oh, man, that sounds nice," you know." And some of those songs, man, when we sang them, they could stand your hair on end, like "Attics of My Life."

DENNIS: Oh, man.
JERRY: Oh, man, that's a gorgeous song, a gorgeous song. And when we sang that, there were times when it was just beautiful, you know, it really was, and I mean, that's something nice to be able to do.

DENNIS: I mentioned living with Hunter, which clearly—you know, those two albums' worth—*Workingman's* and *American Beauty*—

JERRY: Yeah.

DENNIS: —that's a certain kind of peak in terms of material.

JERRY: Oh, yeah.

DENNIS: Incredible stuff.

JERRY: We were doing a lot of stuff. It was fun coming up with that stuff.

DENNIS: As I said, was that a motive on your part just to be a more complete musician?

JERRY: No, not really. *Workingman's Dead* was something very conscious because the idea of that was to be able to go into the studio and do a very simple, unambitious record.

DENNIS: A year before that, in April, for instance, when you got the pedal steel— were you thinking in terms of, "Well, pedal steel sounds interesting. Maybe I'll fool around with it," or—

JERRY: No, nothing with any kind of planning like that. Here's what happened. I'll tell you. It's really very simple.

I'd fooled around a little bit with pedal steels and stuff, but I couldn't make any sense of them. And then we went to a music store in Denver, and there was a completely strung-up, tuned-up, nicely put together, set-up and everything, pedal steel. You know, state-of-the-art ten-stringer, with two necks and everything. And I sat down at it, and I played with the pedals a little bit and I fooled with the tuning. I dug the tuning and I played with the pedals a little. And I said, "Oh, I see!" You know, suddenly I finally started to understand a little of the sense of it, the tuning and the way it worked. And that was the first time I'd ever been near one and I saw how this works, you know. So I said, "I want to buy this fuckin' thing, but can you send it to me with it in tune, you know, 'cause I'll never remember this tuning." So they packed it up and sent it to me in tune. I took it out and unpacked it, and sure enough—it was really the thing of discovering that I could relate to it, because it's very different than a guitar. It's not a guitar, and it's not a banjo, either, you know? It's not like either one of those instruments in any way. And it's only superficially like anything that I played at the time. And it's really very different. It has very different logic to it.

Being in that music store finally, with one correctly tuned and one together the way they're supposed to be, and just a chance to touch it and fool with it for about fifteen minutes, I finally could start to see the sense of it. And seeing the sense of an instrument is the whole instrument. You know what I mean? If you don't understand the logic of an instrument, the sense of an instrument, how it works, what makes it do what it does, you'll never understand the instrument. Never. It would be like picking up a saxophone and, "What is this?" You know?

DENNIS: Right.

JERRY: Somebody has to show you the sense of it, of the fingering . . . Well, the pedal steel is not a self-explanatory instrument by any means, you know. It's a difficult, very strange instrument. It's evolved in strange ways and it has a very singular kind of logic to it. And it is only because of having the glimpse of the interior of the logic of the instrument that made it—because I've always loved the sound of it, and I wanted for years to get one and play one right. I had one, actually, in Ashbury for the longest time. An old cable one. But I didn't have the slightest idea of how to set it up or tune it or anything. So it just sat around and I fucked with it a little bit. I couldn't make any sense of it. It was just totally senseless.

DENNIS: I'm chuckling because, of course, knowing you . . . I mean obviously if you're going to get a flash like that, it's going to be experiential and not consciously thought out.

JERRY: That was the whole thing.

DENNIS: You know—

JERRY: That was exactly what it was.

DENNIS: Get your hands on it and the feel, the inspiration.

JERRY: That's it, getting my hands on it, feeling it. And it was just doing something that I had wanted to do for years, really. Because I wanted to get into pedal steel back when I was playing the banjo. I was attracted to the sound of it on records. "Now there is a snappy sounding instrument. That fucker really sings." But I didn't have the slightest notion of what made it talk, you know, how it worked, or anything like that. And getting my hands on one and just that thing of— the flash. Oh, *yeah*. Like, you know. Really, that's it.

DENNIS: Makes sense.

JERRY: Yeah, really.

The Gamblers.
Airbrush and pen on paper.

DENNIS: Makes sense.

JERRY: It was very obvious, you know, when—

DENNIS: Once you know.

JERRY: Absolutely. It was just the thing of opportunity and time and so forth permitting, you know. It was the thing of finally falling into that place. Because, for one thing, where in the Bay Area can you find a fucking pedal steel, even to this day? I don't even know if you can get one in the Bay Area even now.

DENNIS: Good question.

JERRY: You certainly couldn't back then. So if you wanted to get one, you couldn't even get one in the state of California. I mean, I've been to L.A. They didn't have them down in L.A. You couldn't get them in Bakersfield. As far as I knew, you had to go to Nashville. The only people that made them were one or two small companies that make them kind of the way sports car or racing car companies work. You know what I mean? They make them on—

DENNIS: Small scale.

JERRY: —order. They don't have them sitting around, you know? It's not like that. So that was it. It was really going [to] the part of the country, first of all, where you can find one in a store. That turned out to be the whole story.

>>> <<<

One of the iconic moments of 1969 was the Light Artist Guild strike—a small affair that was significant only in how it revealed the unraveling of what had once seemed a music community. Bill Graham's performance with Stephen Gaskin (a major personality in the Haight-Ashbury scene, who later led a number of people from San Francisco to establish a commune in Tennessee called The Farm) took place at a community meeting held at the Family Dog on the Great Highway a few days after the strike, when Garcia refused to cross the picket line.

DENNIS: We're in the spring of '69, now. All this weird acid stuff is happening and right about this time in March of '69, as it happened, they started trying to put together the Wild West Festival, which ultimately crashed and burned. And out of that came the Light Artist Guild and that abortive strike, which ended up with you and Rock and, I don't know, Chet and a guy from the Light Guild and whatnot and maybe other people, too, in a truck in the parking lot. And then Bill Graham's most famous, masterful performance as flying asshole.

JERRY: He was brilliant.

DENNIS: A truly brilliant performance as ultimate asshole.

JERRY: "You slimy little man." Whoa, you know? And then a brick came through the window right as he was doing that. It was incredible, it really was. It was, like all of a sudden, whoa, the earthquake, y'know? Oh, shit. Bill put out more energy—I don't think I've ever seen him either perform so well or get so incredibly furious. It was Steve Gaskin—he just blew up. He tore his head off.

DENNIS: "You could have had money or love, Bill. You took the money. Don't ask for love now."

JERRY: Right. "You slimy little . . . " Yeah, then it was, "Don't get peaceful with me." That was it.

DENNIS: Right. "Don't touch me, motherfucker."

JERRY: Gaskin said, "I saw the play and it was better." Bill lifted that line from some play, although I don't know what it is.

DENNIS: [*laughing*] That, I didn't know.

JERRY: Yeah. That line, the one about "Don't get peaceful with me."

DENNIS: Oh, thank you. I mean, I know it's a performance, it's always a performance, but to know that—

JERRY: Yeah.

DENNIS: That's great.

JERRY: Either a movie or a play or something. But Gaskin pinned him, Gaskin had him figured out. It was funny shit, you know, it really was. That was all really pathetic stuff. The Light Show people had no business going on strike.

DENNIS: Oh, no, it was silly.

JERRY: People didn't go to those things to see the light shows.

DENNIS: Quote. This is from Jerry [Abrams, leader of the Light Artists Guild strike] recently: "I had assurances from Jerry Garcia that he would honor our line, not that the Dead necessarily would, but that he would."

JERRY: Right.

DENNIS: "Chet knew about it in advance. Everybody knew. We never restrained anyone, physically, from entering . . . They went in—"

JERRY: Except Mickey and Jerry—

DENNIS: Right. So you weren't restrained—

JERRY: I did it because of my union background, I think, really, you know? Just because all my life I've been respecting unions, the SUP across the street, my grandmother and the Laundry Workers Union—I was a union person. I was raised in a union family. I mean, just the idea of any kind of union was something that, you know.

DENNIS: I hadn't even thought of that, frankly.

JERRY: That was really the only reason. Not because of any particular loyalty toward the Light Show people or toward Jerry Abrams or anybody else—

DENNIS: I'd forgotten that. Thank you.

JERRY: —but just being a respecter of the unionization thing. You know? It's just part of my background. I'm reluctant to cross a picket line now.

Jerry with Robert Hunter, 1962.

DENNIS: Oh, yeah. Me too.

JERRY: Even though the union movement, such as it is in the United States, is pretty defunct.

DENNIS: Not quite got the same zip it once had.

JERRY: It certainly doesn't. I mean, and I'm a member of the musicians union, which I think is one of the all-time bad jokes of all time, you know what I mean? Musicians union is really silly. But it's like a reflex, you know?

Jerry on Robert Hunter

The Grateful Dead would not have been what it was without Robert Hunter. If anyone doubts that, let them listen to the lyrics of a few Dead songs before Hunter arrived to add literacy—brilliant art in words—to their compositions. With the single exception of Bob Weir's "Other One," prior to Hunter, you're stuck with songs like "Cream Puff War"—not exactly a literary masterpiece. By turns openhearted and curmudgeonly, Hunter was the secret ingredient of the Grateful Dead sauce. By the time Hunter and his partner Christie moved in with Garcia and Mountain Girl in their home in Larkspur in early 1969, they'd already been writing together for two years and had produced masterpieces like "Dark Star" and "St. Stephen." This new and ongoing proximity propelled their already fruitful artistic partnership to an entirely new level.

The arc of this conversation moves from Hunter and his favorite flower, roses, to how the two of them worked together, to a consideration of a couple of their classic songs, "Ripple" and "Mission in the Rain," and what Jerry did and didn't feel comfortable singing.

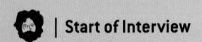 | **Start of Interview**

JERRY: Hunter's got a lyric thing about roses. I don't know whether he picked it up from that or whether it's his own trip, but it's as natural to him as anything else.

DENNIS: From the fact that he's a relation to Robert Burns.
JERRY: Yeah.

M. G.: The rose and thistle?
JERRY: That whole "Annie laid her head down in the roses" ["It Must Have Been the Roses"] is right out of Robert Burns, lifted pretty much whole.

DENNIS: He says the same thing in another interview, Hunter does, "You know, beauty and short-livedness and thorns and odor and everything is the metaphor for life, what's better?"
JERRY: Yeah. The roses.

>>> <<<

DENNIS: Do you see any comparison with that [Lenny Bruce's way with language; see "Jerry on Lenny Bruce," page 90] with Hunter's way of language?

JERRY: Yeah. Hunter is able to do it methodically. Hunter is able to do it on purpose and methodically and out here. And he's able to manipulate it. You know? He is so skillful at that, and he is the only guy I know that can do that kind of stuff. And when Hunter and I write a song together, I can tell Hunter where I want the vowels and consonants, you know, and what kind of vowels I want, and he can write to order like that, you know?

DENNIS: Far out.

JERRY: And still make it make sense and still make it be good. And that is not easy.

DENNIS: Oh, no. No. He scrambled my brain when he played for me the work tape you gave him for "Uncle John's Band."

JERRY: Yeah.

DENNIS: Now, the thing is, this is in the great transition of the Grateful Dead, and it's spring '69, and the work tape is some basic changes, but it's mid-'69 Grateful Dead, which means badass electric, intense, it goes on twenty minutes, it's just this open jam.

JERRY: Yeah.

DENNIS: Now, for almost anybody else, our universal first primal take on "Uncle John's Band" is, of course, the acoustic version on the record.

JERRY: Right.

DENNIS: 'Cause I don't know if you played it in public before you recorded it.

JERRY: No.

DENNIS: I don't think so. But anyway—to me, you know, it's the classic example of the words and the music fitting flawlessly.

JERRY: Yeah.

DENNIS: And then I'm going, "How did he hear those words?"

JERRY: Right.

DENNIS: Which seemed so perfect in those really intense psychedelic electric changes, you know, real spacey.

JERRY: Yeah, right. Well, you had to be there. You know what I mean? And also, you had to be able to get all the intent. Which is a lot of the communication that I would communicate to Hunter. Stuff like that, the intent. And then he'd come back and say, "Well, is this it?" And I'd say, no, it's a little more like that, or this one is it, but these aren't. You know?

DENNIS: Yeah.

JERRY: And sometimes it would be very funny, but he's so easy to work with. God, I couldn't hope to work with a guy that was more perfect. Plus, he has the ability to say what I would have wanted to say. I mean, sometimes I can read things and he can write for me from my point of view so effortlessly . . . I'm as transparent to him as a windowpane, I'm sure. He knows me so well, you know. [*laughter*]

〉〉〉 〈〈〈

DENNIS: The lyrics to "Ripple" among other things—

JERRY: Yeah.

DENNIS: —are like, perfect things.

JERRY: In their way they're perfect, I guess. "Ripple" is a little talky even for me.

DENNIS: Really?

JERRY: Whenever I sing that song, there is a moment or two [when] I feel like, am

211

I really a Presbyterian minister? You know what I mean? It just—it crowds me just a little. It's right within range. I mean, I can just manage it, but if it were . . . if it had one more—

DENNIS: One more word—
JERRY: Right. If it had one more cautionary moment in it, or whatever that is—

DENNIS: Uh huh.
JERRY: Yeah, I'd have real problems with it.

DENNIS: I know what you're saying.
JERRY: I personally have a real low embarrassment level.

DENNIS: Join the crew—yes, I understand.
JERRY: And certain words, I just can't make them come out of my mouth. You know what I mean?

DENNIS: As a matter of fact, Hunter remarked that the song "If I Had the World to Give" was unusual for you. It was overly emotional and I'm not surprised you didn't play it very often.
JERRY: That's true.

DENNIS: It's a little more—bold.
JERRY: There are certain kinds of songs—I mean, there's no logic to my selection, because I sing songs that are really personal. I sing a few songs that, at least to me, feel very exposed.

DENNIS: Hunter-Garcia songs?
JERRY: Yeah, sure.

DENNIS: Like what?
JERRY: Oh, like "Walking Along in the Mission in the Rain," for example.

DENNIS: Yeah, okay.

JERRY: It's like really sort of an autobiographical song. Hunter is able to write me, you know?

DENNIS: Sure.

JERRY: And he's able to say things. He's able to put things into my mouth that I would like to have thought I could say. But sometimes they feel awful close to me, and so some songs I can't always sing. Sometimes I feel a little too raw to sing them. I mean, it's just … it's really quirky and it's not consistent, either, because sometimes the songs don't seem to have anything to do with me. It's just one of those things. The point is that as far as that goes, anything that's at all weird, I have trouble singing it. I mean, weird from my point of view. It's hard for me to know exactly what that is. It's hard for me to lie in a song, you know what I mean?

DENNIS: Which is good. I appreciate—

JERRY: I can act a little, but I can't lie.

DENNIS: When you sing other people's lyrics, I would say … I mean, there are things that you can sing, you know, romantic or directly, overtly sexual, you know what I mean? Something that if Marvin Gaye wrote it, you can act it because it's okay.

JERRY: Or Smokey Robinson.

DENNIS: Or Smokey.

JERRY: Sure. I can sing somebody else's [lyrics]. I don't mind that kind of stuff at all, but on the other hand, Hunter is able to write sensitive stuff like Dylan stuff. Sometimes I can sort of be that persona that Dylan's songs come out of, and I know it's not really quite me, but it's somebody that I know. It's like something I know. Or there's something about me that that song has something to do with. It's an emotional thread, more than logical. It doesn't even have to do with content. Sometimes it's just a feeling. Mostly it's just a feeling. It's tough for me to … I don't think about the songs the way Hunter does. Sometimes I don't even get the sense of them for a long time.

DENNIS: Yeah, you were saying that [in] an interview.

JERRY: Yeah, there are a couple of songs that I sang for the longest time without ever understanding what the lyrics were about. I mean, literally, you know? And then finally, "oh, far out." I either read them or I listened to them or something and then all of a sudden it flashed in my [mind]—"oh, goddamn." You know?

DENNIS: They're subtle. I'll tell you that much.

JERRY: Sometimes they are.

DENNIS: Sometimes. I just had a flash as I was driving out here. I am not into literary close analysis. I never have been. I managed to do a book about Kerouac without getting into it, but there is something about "Uncle John's Band" that I just—I was driving along one night and got into some funny place when I started tearing the song apart. It focused on the four questions that are asked: Will you come with me? Where does the time go? Where does the song go? How does the song go? All that.

JERRY: Yeah.

DENNIS: There are some subtleties to that work that I had no notion of, but what intrigued me is that that is as anthemic as the Grateful Dead has ever been towards their audience. And there is one other song that I flashed on this afternoon that directly invites the hearer along. You know, "Will you come with me?" ["Uncle John's Band."]

JERRY: Yeah.

DENNIS: And that is, oddly enough, the other sort of anthem, which is "Dark Star."

JERRY: Yeah.

DENNIS: It's "shall we go"—

JERRY: Yeah.

DENNIS: —"into the—"

JERRY: "You and I, while we can."

DENNIS: "While we can." And after fifteen years of listening, it struck me that that's very interesting. I haven't thought it out yet, but—

JERRY: Well, I'll tell you that as a writer I've had ideas where I thought I want to write a song that addresses the situation as it's really happening, that is to say, the experience of standing onstage and playing to this huge group of people in real time.

DENNIS: Uh huh. And?

JERRY: I would like to have a song that addresses that. You know? And I've had a few ideas that I thought were going to be that, but then they didn't turn out to be that. "Wharf Rat" was one of them and— "Terrapin" was one of them.

DENNIS: You had that thought before you saw Hunter's lyrics?

JERRY: Yeah. I had a whole melody. I had the instrumental part of it worked out, just came to me all at once. It was one of those songs that came to me all at once. But what I was thinking of when it came to me was, jeez, it would be great to have a song that was like, now it's that moment onstage when we could all look at each other and say, okay, here we are. We're in the now. Here we are in the now. Let's address this situation as it's happening in the now. You know? It was like writing a song that addresses that somehow, although how to do it without it being a total bullshit trip was something that totally escaped me. I don't know what I would want to say apart from isn't it great to be here and isn't it swell that we're all here?

It's like, I know the power of that moment. You know? That there is a certain moment. And, I mean, I've tried to write some songs, all stuff that's manipulate-able. Although I'm not that great at manipulating it. Other rock 'n' roll people really are. But it's one of those things that—you know, all the formulas in rock 'n' roll, the stuff that having the band doing big riffs together and stops and, you know, all the things you do for dramatic emphasis.

215

All the different things that you can do, changing, modulating, changing keys and doing things up a half step and stuff that builds incredible tension. Those are tricks, really, that work—but once you've used them, you realize they're tricks and they're basically manipulative and so the fun goes out of them almost immediately. The idea is you want to do something that you don't know what it's going to be and it also has that kind of effect. Or an effect that you haven't experienced before. So that, trying to write songs that are both tight and loose at the same time, that's the kind of thing that I used to try to do. I haven't tried it for a long time, because now I sort [of] have gone back to—I've got some tunes that I'm working on right now. Hunter just gave me some new lyrics.

And my feeling about songwriting now is somewhere back where it was about the time we did *Workingman's Dead*, not that I'm going to write those kinds of songs, but the idea that the song is the thing. You've got to forget about the situation. Just make the song work.

So in that sense, I never have succeeded in doing that thing of writing the song that was big. I wanted to write a song that's big, as big as the situation is. I could never pull it off, at least not yet. Some songs have grown to that size.

"Not Fade Away" is a fabulous song . . . and I loved it when it was a rock 'n' roll—I mean, I loved it when I was a kid, and doing it now almost always gives me a thrill. It stands my hair on end. It's just a great song.

8

Two Final Episodes

Point of Light.
Pen and ink on paper.

The three nights of performance in September 1978, in front of the Great Pyramid of Giza, Egypt, were among the great moments in Dead history. Garcia falling into a diabetic coma in 1986 had to rank among the worst.

In the mid-'70s, the Dead's manager, Richard Loren, had visited Egypt. Having discovered a small stage meant for "Sound and Light" shows at the base of the Great Pyramid, he had the idea of getting the Dead to come to Egypt and play at the pyramids. It became his mission, and in the fall of 1978, after meeting with various Egyptian heavies, including the minister of culture, they were able to fulfill Loren's dream.

In July 1986, shortly after returning home from some murderously hot and humid concerts at RFK Stadium in Washington, D.C., a severely dehydrated Jerry went into a week-long diabetic coma, which he refers to here as a "meltdown." It's not clear how close to death he came, but it was certainly a scary time for all.

 | Start of Interview

DENNIS: . . . what you must have felt when the moon went into eclipse in Egypt.

JERRY: I was just happy to be there. I didn't—it wasn't anything special. It was—the whole thing of being there was just so incredibly neat. It was different than what I expected, but it was much neater on many levels, and farther out on many levels. When the eclipse started, Healy and I were the only ones on stage. [Dan Healy was the band's sound mixer for much of its career, with a significant influence on the development of their sound.] We were out there by ourselves; it was before the show. It was kind of an awkward time of night, you know? It was a little too early to start playing. So the band wasn't there, just Healy and I. We kind of played a little, you know, played the moon into darkness. And then the kids in the village do this thing, which they do whenever there is an eclipse. They go out to scare the darkness away, whatever it is. And they come through the village making all these little noises and sounds and all this stuff. It sounded really neat. And just being out there, with the Great Pyramid behind you and the Sphinx alongside. Shit, you know? If there was a moment and a place and a time to be somewhere, this is the place. This is the time. This is the moment. You know? It was like the thing of being able to appreciate that pretty fully, and I sure enjoyed it. I didn't have anything special in mind, but—I mean, what we were doing

Jerry Garica at Saqqara Pyramid in Giza, Egypt, September 1978.

was not lost on the people who were there. I remember this Egyptian guy came up to me and asked me if I had seen *Close Encounters of the Third Kind.* I said, yeah. He says, yes, it's like the music, the music and the Great Pyramid and the saucers, and he had this whole thing already—this whole fantasy already spun, you know? And to me, it was like, just one of those things where it was like, maybe, the best fantasy that anybody ever had about the Grateful Dead and we were actually—

DENNIS: Doing it.
JERRY: I was only sorry we didn't play better. We really didn't play that good.

DENNIS: No.
JERRY: But just being there was fabulous.

DENNIS: Yeah, yeah. Well, that was the justification.
JERRY: Yes.

DENNIS: It was such a far-out thing to do. I was sitting there at home just being proud of you for doing something so totally insane, so totally—

JERRY: It was a perfect moment in its way, and we sure had a great fuckin' time. I mean, people said, "Why did you pay to do that?" You know what I mean?

DENNIS: What better thing to spend money on?

JERRY: Right. It was like, man, if you could pay to have that much fun, it doesn't matter how much you have to pay. To have that much fun is definitely fucking worth it, you know? It was one of those things I'll never regret. That was a magical moment, it really was.

〉〉〉 〈〈〈

**Garcia's descent into a diabetic coma in 1986 was
a low point in the band's story.**

JERRY: I've had a lot of chance to reflect these last—

DENNIS: Yeah.

JERRY: —ever since my meltdown

DENNIS: Yeah.

JERRY: And I mean, it's just—I've been just thinking about stuff, mostly tracking things down because . . . I came out of that kinda scrambled.

〉〉〉 〈〈〈

JERRY: Hey, listen man, I tell ya. I mean, I've got a lot of gaps. Well, they're kind of funny kind of gaps . . . I have to hunt for words now and again. That's still something I notice. My random access is a little strange, but, yeah, I was talking some completely personal kind of symbolic gibberish when I came out of that coma.

And it was really weird, you know? It was strange from my point of view because I understood what it was that I was trying to say, but I couldn't make anybody understand me. It was peculiar. It took a day or so for that to sort of shake down, but since then it's been the thing of collecting what I know and what I don't know, what I can do. I don't miss what I don't know, you know, or what I—whatever I don't remember, I don't miss it because it's not there.

DENNIS: Have you identified what it is that you don't remember?
JERRY: No. I bump into things.

DENNIS: Right.
JERRY: It's the very nature of not remembering.

DENNIS: Exactly. I've just been reading Julian Jaynes [philosopher and author of *The Origin of Consciousness in the Breakdown of the Bicameral Mind*] again—not again, but taking another stab at it.
JERRY: Yeah.

DENNIS: And all that you know, that's the thing, you don't know what you don't know.
JERRY: When it's gone, it's gone. And what I may have known . . . I mean, in a way I'm sort of a different person. The material is all there, but every once in a while I run into a blank. Like working down in the studio, every once in a while I look at something and I know what it is and I know that I know that I've used it and I know that it has a name and I know that somewhere I know the name, but usually I have to get somebody, "Hey, what do you call this thing again?" You know? And then, like that, there is some of that kind of stuff, but it's kind of like all of the material in my mind kind of got thrown into one place and stirred up, you know? It's kind of like that.

DENNIS: That, presumably, as the cellular structure your body realigns to health—
JERRY: Yes. Something like that. I really don't know. The way I understand it is that when you're real sick, your blood tries to protect your brain. It leaves every

Irish Tree.
Watercolor on paper.

place else and heads for your brain in an effort to sort of gather around there, so that you—I guess you don't lose too much neural imprinting or whatever you've got or however you remember stuff, and it's been strange. Coming out of it has been real strange. And it was weird while it was happening. I mean, I lost about four, about five days, maybe, a week.

DENNIS: Really?

JERRY: About a week. Yeah. They're gone. I don't know how I got to the hospital. I don't know any of that stuff.

DENNIS: What you've lost starts from, like, that afternoon or something.

JERRY: I guess so. Yeah. I really—

DENNIS: I mean, like, you remember D.C. [concerts at RFK Stadium in Washington, D.C., on July 6 and 7, 1986] and coming back?

JERRY: Yeah, sure, it's not until—I mean, when I woke up in the hospital. I don't know when—I remember a couple of times kinda surfacing. You know?

DENNIS: Yeah, like a dream?

JERRY: Tubes and everything, you know, and I didn't understand where I was or what was happening . . . so I went back under, kind of. It was strange, though. It was—from my point of view, I was involved in some kind of furious conflict and tremendous activity, but I don't know what it was. It had a kind of science fiction-y quality.

DENNIS: It's a coma. I mean, that's the essence of a coma, really.

JERRY: Yeah. I really don't know. I picked up a lot of weird little things on the way out, you know? Coming out of the coma, that in-between part is the only

part I can really relate to because the main part of it is just gone—I don't
know what happened. It's been strange.

DENNIS: Yeah.
JERRY: I didn't know how sick I was.

DENNIS: Yeah.
JERRY: Weird experience.

DENNIS: Yeah, truly. Nice to be on the other side of.
JERRY: Yeah. Right. It's nice to have come away from it really clean. I mean, I don't
have to take insulin.

DENNIS: That's a fabulous thing.
JERRY: Or any of that kind of crap. I'm pretty lucky.

223

DENNIS: One of the doctors had said that you
were the toughest mother —I mean,
structurally—that he'd ever—I mean,
could not believe that you walked away
on the terms that you did.
JERRY: Yeah.

DENNIS: It was like you had— It was a long shot.
JERRY: Yeah.

DENNIS: I said the same thing about my mother,
as a matter of fact. She was a skinny little
nothing who just—
JERRY: Lucky for sturdy genes, you know. That's
one of those things you can be thankful
that your parents were selective or not, you
know, or whatever fortunate fallout …

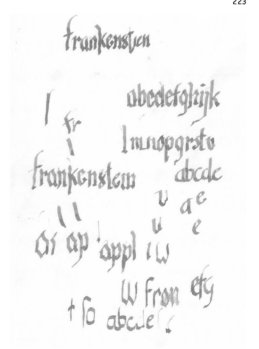

Frankenstein Calligraphy.

"And some of those songs, man, when we sang them, they could stand your hair on end."

Yeah. I never felt like I was in any personal danger. I mean, personally, you know? I didn't find out until later that I was in any danger at all, really. When I came out of it, I didn't know how sick I was or how sick they thought I was.

DENNIS: Right.
JERRY: Any of that crap—luckily I missed all that shit.

DENNIS: Really.
JERRY: I certainly didn't mean to scare everybody.

DENNIS: Absolutely. Well, all I can say is that night as Susana [Millman, Dennis's wife, a noted photographer of the Dead] and I were sitting there looking at each other going, ummm, she did the neatest possible thing, which was she got up and she went to last year's Ventura shows, that being in our forefront, and put on "Touch of Grey."

224

And as a matter of fact about two days later I was talking with Hunter on the phone—he was at the hospital—and I started quoting him his own song, and it was as though he hadn't written it. He sort of did this take and went, "Oh, yeah, right. That's true. That's true." But it . . . was almost as though he was shocked that someone was quoting him back to him.
JERRY: Yeah, you don't expect it.

≫≫ ≪≪

JERRY: Hunter was one of the first guys that I was coherently—I mean, not coherent—

DENNIS: —aware of. As it should be, somehow.
JERRY: I told him I wasn't crazy. I mean, that was the gist. I had a message for him. I told him, "Hey, Hunter, if I die tomorrow or if I die before anybody gets a chance to talk to me, tell 'em I wasn't crazy, man." [*laughter*] It seemed

important at the time, although I don't remember exactly what I had in my mind. It seemed important.

M. G.: It was important. You were having a reality check. You were having a hard time being here. At that time.

JERRY: Well, I didn't understand it.

M. G.: No—your dreams, they weren't leaving you alone yet.

JERRY: No, they sure as shit weren't.

Jerry snorkeling in Kauai, 1988.

DENNIS: That's the thing with coma.

M. G.: Oh, man, it was trouble.

DENNIS: I was checking out Krippner's [Dr. Stanley Krippner, a friend of the band and distinguished researcher in states of consciousness] list of the various states of consciousness. There were a lot more—there were like nine or eleven or something. It's not just the beta and the alpha and that, but it's like sleep and dreaming and, you know, various stages within sleep.

JERRY: Mm-hmm.

DENNIS: Coma is like sort of number nine or something, right? You know?

JERRY: It's out there, man, I'll tell ya.

Jerry on Sätty, Scotty Stoneman, and Bill Keith

Jerry had an exquisite appreciation for other artists, of whatever medium. Wilfried "Sätty" Podriech was a German-born avant-garde artist who came to San Francisco in the 1960s. Though he did some posters, he ran in different circles from Garcia. Some of his best-known work included projects like "The Annotated Dracula" and "The Illustrated Poe." Shortly after the Grateful Dead helped close Winterland (their last show there was on December 31, 1978), Sätty approached Jerry and invited Jerry to his home and studio near Fisherman's Wharf for a conversation. The visual detail Jerry summons up from his one encounter with Sätty is simply astonishing.

And it seems natural to end these interviews with Jerry's thoughts on Scotty Stoneman, the fiddle player for the Kentucky Colonels, a bluegrass group of Jerry's own generation (although Scotty was a decade older). Jerry's enthusiasm and engagement in this discussion were at an all-time high (and that's saying something!). In the middle of speaking about Scotty, he breaks off to consider his debt to Bill Keith, a young banjo player whose playing taught Jerry a great deal.

| Start of Interview

DENNIS: You talked about how you met Sätty once—"One graphic artist turned me on to a whole level of what the G.D. does that I wasn't even cognizant of . . ."

JERRY: Yeah. Yeah. That was a high point.

DENNIS: "He took me to the house and turned me on—prints," and showed you stuff. I would like to go look at what he showed you. Can you describe—?

JERRY: Sure, I know—they were made from, what's-his-name, Bob Seidemann's Pigpen poster. You know that Pigpen shot of his? Remember, the neat shot—

DENNIS: Yeah. Yeah.

JERRY: —and the table.

DENNIS: Right.

JERRY: Yeah. There's a table. Kinda angular.

DENNIS: On the table—

JERRY: They have kind of a—

DENNIS: With the black biker hat.

JERRY: Dark glasses, and he looks kind of strange. And these were sort of made using that as a basic element . . . Sätty was a real clever printmaker. That was one of the things he did. And so he had all these different colors and different shapes sort of melting into them—and they were all basically posters of Pigpen, essentially, but each one was pretty different. They were in a big stack like this.

I could identify them in a minute— because they really made an impression on me. And mostly, his talk about how when he went to a Grateful Dead show, sometimes the music made him feel sick. Sometimes it gave him a headache, you know? Sometimes it scared him. Sometimes it made him laugh. Sometimes it made him sing. He was an interesting guy because he had—he was one of those guys with what he described as a first-class European education. You know, one of those guys that went to the German Academies, you know what I mean? He was like an interesting guy. He's German, Polish. You know? That border. German, Polish descent. And he had been through some interesting things. He told me all about himself. And he also had an incredible occult book collection, including, like, a Gutenberg in middle German, which he could read—a Gutenberg *Paracelsus.* And, I mean, he blew me away.

DENNIS: Yeah. Well, that's authentically far out.

JERRY: The way he had his whole life organized and his environment, the place he lived in, the way it was organized—you climb down this ladder and the whole basement of his place, which is on the old sand dunes, you know, it was like down near Fisherman's Wharf. He had a storefront. And you climbed down the stairs that were on sand dunes and he put, like, a whole lot of polyvinyl chloride and then Persian carpets over it. It was like

227

rolling—and it was like this huge room that ran the length of the house. And there were two rooms off the side of it, and one had big couches and looked through a one-way mirror into this other room that had a low, huge, circular table with every conceivable liqueur you've ever seen on it and a million candles. And around it were great big incredible ornate easy chairs, each one different from the other, where you could sit around and talk, you know? It was a room for sitting around and talking. And then there was a room off of it where you could watch. It was incredible.

DENNIS: [*much laughter*] It was a work of art itself.

JERRY: And then there was another place—you climbed up a little ladder and he had this tall, skinny, weird architectural accident room that had a high light source. The light came down and he had, like, one of those medieval desks, you know, a tall desk that you can sit at with a stool.

DENNIS: Oh, the script—

JERRY: Yeah. One of those kinds of jobs. And he had his *Paracelsus* out on it and rusty swords and sabers and shit in the corner, muskets and all this stuff, and it was like his library. And he had all his occult books and they seemed to go on to infinity. I mean, he had the whole place tuned environmentally. And his main thing as he went into the storefront, it was like a combination kitchen alcove and a big bright table with lots of chairs around it where you could sit and drink coffee and bullshit.

DENNIS: Right.

JERRY: And he had his drawing tables and his art stuff there so he could catch the light from the windows. And it was—I mean, his whole scene was so tuned and his mind was so elegant. You know what I mean? He turned me on in a night to millions of ideas. I'm still mulling them over, you know? He was an amazing guy. I mean, he really was a turn on. Difficult guy, I could tell.

DENNIS: He had a weird reputation.

M. G.: He was real sensitive.

JERRY: Yeah, he had a weird reputation. And I never got—I never hung out with him more than that one time, really, except one other time, I think, maybe I fell in with him briefly, but he introduced the idea of full-range to me, which was actually always there in Grateful Dead music, but he was the first one that enunciated that concept, and it was something that he appreciated as an artist, I mean. And he wanted me to know since that was the last show at Winterland—he wanted me to know what it meant to him, you know? It was a fascinating experience, really a fascinating guy, too. Sorry he's dead. He's another guy that I'm sorry he's dead. I don't know what he died of—

DENNIS: It was natural, but I forget what.

M. G.: Like a brain tumor or a neurological disease kind of thing.

JERRY: He was a brain tumor guy.

〉〉〉 〈〈〈

DENNIS: In one interview, you once remarked that you got a number of guitar ideas from Scotty Stoneman.

JERRY: Oh, yeah. Well, Scotty Stoneman was one of those guys that opened up music, you know, because he'd start off with a tune, a fiddle tune like "Blackberry Blossom" or some fiddle tune [*singing*],and he'd take that sucker out, I mean, and it would be like twenty minutes would go by. And he was playing ideas that went across four choruses, you know. Instead of playing the tune, it would be some crazed idea that stretched all the way across it. I mean, he was like the Coltrane of country fiddle, really. Have you ever heard him play?

DENNIS: [No]—I –

JERRY: I'll have to find you some tapes of him playing really outside. I mean, he played so soulfully. His playing had so much pain—beautiful, you know. And, plus, incredible sensibilities, man. I mean, the incredible freshness and neatness of his ideas are just—oh! I mean, he's played some of the coolest solos in bluegrass music, bar none, you know what I mean? Some of them are so fresh and so exciting—I'll have to play you my [record]. I've got one record somewhere. It's a reissue of the Kentucky Colonels where I do the intro. I do a live intro from a show that I put on of them and when Scott Stoneman was playing for them. There's two or three tunes on there … when I heard him play, he was sick. He was dying. He died from drinking hair tonic, you know. He's one of those guys that was an alcoholic by the time he was fourteen or fifteen.

DENNIS: Yeah, another Pig.
JERRY: And he died from drinking hair tonic. And when I heard him play, he was sick and dying, in fact. And man, his playing was so gorgeous. And I knew guys that learned from him. Richard Greene, that fiddler, learned from him. And he'd ask Scotty how he played something. Scotty would just say, "I just play it lonesome, man. I just play it lonesome." Beautiful.

DENNIS: It's interesting, because your predecessor, at least when you were playing banjo, I think you would acknowledge that one of the guys you were super conscious of was Bill Keith—
JERRY: Oh, sure.

DENNIS: —simply because he was the city guy who made it into the real bluegrass world.
JERRY: Right.

DENNIS: And, of course, his trip was, you know, playing fiddle on a banjo.
JERRY: Yeah. And what I liked more than that was the wonderful sense of rhythmic intuition and syncopation that he had in his playing that was more subtle—it was in his rolls. And his fiddle stuff—I didn't get off on that that much, although I learned it, of course. But it was his other stuff that knocked me out. I mean, he had a fantastic way of playing things that syncopated in surprising ways and went on and on, but did it really gracefully. Boy, he had some cool backup. His backup playing—the playing that's not out front that he did was what was really a knockout, boy. I

listened through the singing to what he was doing and all—oh, my God, listen to that guy. Shoo.

That's what I really learned from. I learned the gesture of his playing, you know. Something else—I don't even know exactly what it is, but the thing of being able to extend ideas a little more and to have a fresh notion of how to syncopate things and that. He did it—I don't know where he got that stuff, but boy, it was so cool, you know? He brought something to banjo playing for me. I mean, he influenced me in another way much more than that, solos and that fiddle style.

DENNIS: Uh huh.

JERRY: Although the fiddle style was important, for me the other part of his banjo playing was—because it was more like the traditional [Earl] Scruggs style in a sense, you know, but it had another thing altogether. Actually, other banjo players didn't pick up on it. It's a little detail of his playing that kind of missed the boat, you know, that other guys didn't catch.

DENNIS: And it basically comes out of rhythm.

JERRY: Yeah, that's what I feel—that's what it belongs to. It's just where you place the notes. Where you put them rhythmically and that, you know? It's something that's affected my playing much more, even. I mean, it's still in my guitar playing, and I hear it even if nobody else [does]—even if I could never trace it down, I hear it, you know.

DENNIS: Well, what you just said is in a sense a rewrite of a paragraph that I wrote about Kerouac and Parker, and actually, Jackson Pollock—

JERRY: Right you are.

DENNIS: —in which the response to the modern post–World War II world was—and again—and it's the natural consequence of going into improvisation and into the intuitive—is you can't necessarily on the intuitive level—well, when it all blows away, rhythm is what's going to take you there.

JERRY: It was that bebop thing. For them it was that bebop thing. You're right about that. It's the same sort of thing.

DENNIS: The thing is, Monroe's bluegrass is, to me, speaking as a cultural historian, exactly the same thing as Charlie Parker—

JERRY: It's white bebop.

DENNIS: It's white bebop. It's taking the basic old stuff, the pop music, gospel, blah, blah, blah, and speeding it up.

JERRY: That's right. The only thing it doesn't have is the harmonic richness of bebop. You know what I mean? That's what it's missing, but it has everything else. It really does.

DENNIS: It went in the direction of the voice—

JERRY: And the fiddle. Well, like, the fiddle playing and the guy like—well, Scotty Stoneman was an example of it. He was like the Charlie Parker of country fiddle, you know what I mean? I'll play some stuff for you sometime and you'll hear it. You will not believe it. It is out there. You know, what would happen, he would be playing these fiddle tunes, and pretty soon every musician on the stage would be standing there going *ding, ding*. Their instruments would, like, turn to water. You know, they'd stop playing almost entirely and they'd just be listening to Scotty, and he would be sawing away, man, and I mean, things would be coming out of there . . . They're like those incredible excursions Coltrane and those guys took where all of a sudden you're hearing traffic on the streets and people hollering back and forth . . . you know what I mean?

With Scotty it was diesel trucks and the highway. And geese flying from Canada, and I mean *everything*, you know? It's *all* there, and just—oh, man, and *burning* like a forest fire, you know? Never stopping to take a breath. Just [sounding] like a fiddle can be so relentless. When he played, it would go on for twenty minutes, and you would be standing there . . . in fact, the model for getting high musically for me was the thing of being in the audience and listening to Scotty play. Not so much his notes, but that experience, you know—the thing of hearing somebody play their heart out, you know? It's just, oh, shoo—

232

The Volcanic Tree.
Mixed media on paper.

Image Credits

©Adrian Boot
p. 219

©Allen Ginsberg/CORBIS
p. 134

The Estate of David Gahr/Premium Archive/Getty Images
pp. 117, 137

Grateful Dead Archive, UC Santa Cruz
p. 141

©Herb Greene
pp. 2, 8, 94, 152, 161, 167, 191

Jerry Garcia Family Archives, Carolyn Garcia Archives, and Clifford Garcia Archives
pp. 7, 18, 20, 22, 23, 24, 30, 32, 37, 39, 41, 44, 49, 50, 51 (top and bottom), 53, 55 (top and bottom), 57, 58, 60, 63, 65, 66, 68, 74, 78, 86, 87, 98, 99, 104, 106, 109, 119, 120, 127, 128, 132, 142, 149, 150, 153, 156, 177, 178, 179, 188, 194, 197, 199 (top and bottom), 201, 205, 217, 222, 223, 225, 233

©Rosie McGee
p. 193

Courtesy of Rhino Records/Grateful Dead Productions
p. 157

Michael Ochs Archives/Michael Ochs Archives/Getty Images
p. 84

©Roberto Rabanne/RobertoRabanne.com
p. 6, 111, 112, 165

Paul Ryan/Michael Ochs Archives/Getty Images
p. 105

Photographer Unknown
p. 208

©Ted Streshinsky/CORBIS
p. 130

©Iconic Images/Baron Wolman
p. 174

Index

For specific people, see also the
      "Cast of Characters," pp. 13–17.

Page numbers in bold indicate
      photographs or art.

H

I

J

K